CW00506350

WILDFLOWERS&PLANTS

OF CENTRAL AUSTRALIA

WILDFLOWERS&PLANTS

OF CENTRAL AUSTRALIA

ANNE URBAN

PORTSIDE
EDITIONS

PORTSIDE EDITIONS PTY LTD
261 Salmon Street, Fishermens Bend
Victoria, 3207 Australia

First published in Australia 1990 by
PORTSIDE EDITIONS PTY LTD
261 Salmon Street, Fishermens Bend Victoria, 3207 Australia
Reprinted June 1993

Printed by Southbank Pacific Pty Ltd
Melbourne Victoria, Australia

ISBN 0 949318 03 5

Copyright © PORTSIDE EDITIONS PTY LTD

This book is copyright. Apart from any fair dealing for the purposes of private study, research, criticism or review, as permitted under the Copyright Act, no part may be reproduced by any process without written permission. Inquiries should be addressed to the publishers.

CONTENTS

To my husband Victor

and my brother Peter Fannin

ACKNOWLEDGEMENTS

There are several people who have contributed much towards the creation of this book. To them I give special thanks and acknowledgement.

My brother, Peter Fannin, provided the inspiration for the book. He also gave me an enduring love for our Centralian desert plants. The book is based on the experiences I gained in "plant walks" with Peter, and I think of the whole book as one giant "plant walk" through Central Australia.

Without my husband Victor, there would be no book. He first taught me to use a camera, and has guided me from being a raw beginner up to the stage of reasonable proficiency. He has spent hundreds of darkroom hours making colour prints for me. He assisted with my diagrams, and through the years of work he gave me continual encouragement, advice and practical help.

Botanist Greg Leech acted as my science supervisor. He gave many hours of his spare time to correcting my drafts and giving welcome advice. Staff of the N.T. Herbarium, including Greg Leech, Bruce Thompson, and the late John Maconachie, identified all my specimens, and assisted with valuable information.

Mrs Iris Harvey, proprietor of the Arunta Book Store, Alice Springs, gave me the impetus to start, and advice along the way.

I must also pay tribute to all the researchers and writers whose works I have used for reference. A list of these is appended. My principal reference was the *Flora of Central Australia* (1981), ed. J. Jessop. Thanks are also due to those Aboriginal people who have generously shared their knowledge.

Thanks to Mike Fisher, for use of his word processor, and to Shell and Paul Urban for typing assistance.

All my family and countless friends have given me ongoing encouragement. It is not possible to name all, but I make special mention of Mike Gillam, Bill Payne (Editor of 'Australian Plants') and members of the Alice Springs branches of the Society for Growing Australian Plants, and members of the Fellowship of Australian Writers.

Finally, a very special thank you to Rosemary and Alex Coppock of Newhaven Station.

Most of the photographs and diagrams are my own, but I acknowledge with thanks the use of transparencies lent by: Rosemary Coppock: (*Acacia kempeana, Acacia pruinocarpa, Canthium latifolium, Ipomoea costata*); Victor Urban: (*Clianthus formosus, Eucalyptus camaldulensis*); Peter Fannin: (*Gastrolobium brevipes, Wurmbea centralis*).

Thanks also to Maggie Urban, for the diagram of *Crinum flaccidum*.

Anne Urban

Central Australia within the
Northern Territory

The area covered by this book is that between latitudes 20°S and 26°S.

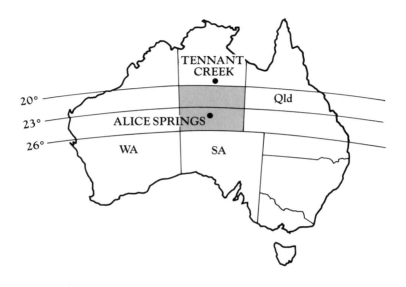

Abbreviations

NT – Northern Territory

CA-NT – Central Australia within the
       Northern Territory

SA – South Australia

Q – Queensland

NSW – New South Wales

Vic – Victoria

WA – Western Australia

PNG – Papua New Guinea

NZ – New Zealand

ssp. – subspecies

var. – variety

INTRODUCTION

Living in Central Australia one becomes fascinated by the ability of plants to survive – and even thrive – in this very hot, dry and arid country. Some years ago I became interested in photographing our local wildflowers. Staff members of the N.T. Herbarium identified the specimens I collected while photographing. Through study and research and help from the experts, I gained enough knowledge to compile this book. The photographs have been taken so as to look lifelike and will be found to be helpful in identification. I hope that readers will not only find the book useful, but also share with me my love of, and endless fascination with, our wild desert plants.

Geographical area covered by the book

This book covers an area which I have called CA-NT. This is that part of Central Australia within the Northern Territory and bounded by latitudes 20° and 26° South (see map on facing page).

Technical terms

When I am reading, I find unfamiliar technical terms very distracting. I have therefore kept such terms to a minimum. Some technical terms are unavoidable. These are explained in an appended glossary.

Botanical names

Plant revision is constantly being undertaken, with many subsequent name changes. Those names used in this book follow the *Checklist of Vascular Plants of the Northern Territory* (April 1987), updated to June 1987.

Common names

Common names have been given when such names have established usage. In using these names I have, for the most part, followed the *Checklist of Preferred Common Names of Plants in the Northern Territory* (B. W. Strong), because common names tend to be very variable.

Order of contents

The order of contents of the book follows that of *The Flora of Central Australia* (1981), and starts with the most primitive plants.

Plant descriptions

This book is not a "Flora". It does not describe all of the species to be found in CA-NT. Plants included consist of those most commonly seen, plus some less common plants which I found especially interesting. For a fuller list of families, genera and species of the N.T., the reader is referred to the *Checklist of Vascular Plants of the Northern Territory* (1987), ed. Dunlop (see references appended). This checklist is constantly being updated by the N.T. Herbarium in Darwin.

The plant descriptions in this book include only the more obvious characteristics of the plant: flower, leaf, fruit, etc. Detailed descriptions can be found in the relevant "Flora".

Measurements

I found it easier to get used to plant sizes by measuring against my own body. Using my personal measurements, 50 cm is knee-high, 1 m is waist-high, 1.5 m is shoulder-high and my arm held vertically above my head reaches just over 2 m. My hand-span is nearly 20 cm, my middle finger 7 cm long, with its nail 1 cm long. As I always carry myself with me, these measurements are a useful guide, and I suggest that readers try it.

Structure of flower and fruit

Flowers may be bisexual, or male or female. Plants with unisexual flowers sometimes have both sexes on the same plant, and sometimes each sex on a different plant. Bisexual flowers contain both the female parts: ovary, style and stigmas, and the male parts: stamens with pollen-containing sacs.

Each flower may or may not have sepals and petals. The sepals may be joined to form a cup. The petals may be joined in many ways.

The seeds develop in the ovary, which develops into "the fruit".

In this book there are some plants which have no flowers. These are ferns, pines and cycads.

One type of bisexual flower, cut longitudinally

Separate male and female flowers (*Dodonaea* species)

PTERIDOPHYTA
(ferns)

Ferns have no seeds or flowers, and may reproduce vegetatively – by suckering, or budding from the roots and stems. They also have a complex sexual life-cycle involving spores. The spores require free water for germination to occur. Therefore ferns are often found at the bottom of rocky gorges and in other places subject to flooding. It has been necessary to limit the number of species described in this book so I have limited the number of ferns, choosing only those which are seen quite often. There are 15 fern families found in CA-NT. Most are only found near permanent water, often in relatively inaccessible places. Sinopteridaceae (rockfern) can be found in low lying areas, at the bottom of rocky slopes, and near waterholes. Marsileaceae (nardoo) is found in and beside water.

Sinopteridaceae (rockfern family)

In CA-NT Sinopteridaceae is represented by several species of *Cheilanthes*.

Genus *Cheilanthes* (rockferns)

Cheilanthes austrotenuifolia and *C. sieberi* (Rockfern)

These two rockferns are very similar and grade into each other. They are found in rocky gorges and at the bottom of rocky outcrops. The fronds (leaves) are usually about 20 cm long, but may be longer in *C. sieberi*. They are mostly hairless. The fruiting bodies develop on the backs of the leaves. In other States, rockfern has a record of being poisonous to both sheep and cattle. This is not a problem in the NT as the fern is usually inaccessible to grazing.

Cheilanthes austrotenuifolia (Rockfern)

11

C. lasiophylla (Woolly cloak-fern)

This small fern is found in rocky areas. The root is a creeping rhizome or underground stem. The leaves form small tufts. Each frond is about 15 cm long and divided into many lobes. The fronds are blue-green with a hairy covering, which is thicker and golden-brown on the back of the leaves.

The fruiting bodies develop on the backs of the leaves and are often hidden amongst the hairs.

Marsileaceae (nardoo family)

Nardoo is a fern. It is found growing in both water and in the mud beside the water. The root is a creeping rhizome or underground stem. The leaves have 4 leaflets on the end of a long stalk. These fronds look rather like a long-stalked four-leafed clover. The leaflets are wedge-shaped and vary from hairless to hairy. The fruiting bodies are on stalks at the base of the plant. They are woody with a ribbed or smooth surface and have a dense hairy covering. They may have up to 2 teeth. Nardoo was an important food item for the Aborigines, who gathered the fruiting bodies and ground them to make cakes. There are 6 species of nardoo found in CA-NT and they are distinguished mainly by the fruiting bodies.

Cheilanthes lasiophylla (Woolly cloak-fern)

Marsilea exarata (Nardoo)

Aboriginal rubbing-stone used for grinding seeds

Marsilea exarata (Nardoo)

Genus *Marsilea* (nardoos)

Marsilea drummondii (Common nardoo)

The CA forms of this nardoo usually have a dense covering of orange-brown hairs. The fronds vary from 2-30 cm long. The fruiting body is 4-9 mm long, and is on a long stalk. It is ribbed and has 2 teeth: 1 triangular and 1 rounded. These so-called 'teeth' are small bumps or knobs at the base of the fruiting body.

Marsilea drummondii – Common nardoo

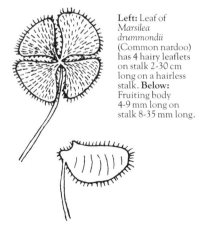

Left: Leaf of *Marsilea drummondii* (Common nardoo) has 4 hairy leaflets on stalk 2-30 cm long on a hairless stalk. **Below:** Fruiting body 4-9 mm long on stalk 8-35 mm long.

GYMNOSPERMAE
(conifers)

Gymnosperms are seed plants with no flowers. The male and female reproductive structures are found in cones, and the seeds are carried unprotected, unlike flowering plants whose seed is enclosed in the fruit.

In the process of evolution, gymnosperms developed after the ferns, but before the flowering plants. There are only 2 gymnosperms found in CA-NT. These are a macrozamia and a cypress pine.

Zamiaceae (cycad family)

Cycads are a very ancient group of plants. There are about 18 species in Australia.

Genus *Macrozamia* (macrozamias)

Macrozamia macdonnellii (MacDonnell Ranges cycad)

This macrozamia occurs only in the MacDonnell and Hartz Ranges where it is found on rocky hillsides and in the gorges. Many of the plants are high up on the walls of the gorges in inaccessible places. Macrozamias are very slow-growing, and those with a large trunk are very old. The fibrous trunk is 1-2 m high and may be partly underground. The long leaves spread out from the top of the trunk and have narrow pointed leathery leaflets 12-17 cm long. As the plant grows the lower leaves wither and form a skirt. There are separate male and female plants. The cones develop at the end of the trunk. Male cones are long and narrower than the female cones. They are 20-40 x 10 cm and consist of spirals of woody plates which carry the pollen cases. The female cones are broader, 20-30 cm in diameter, and contain the female egg cells. These develop into white egg-like seeds which have a bright-red covering. In other parts of Australia Aborigines ate the starchy cycad seeds – after first treating them to leach out the poison. There is no record of them doing this in CA-NT.

M. macdonnellii – ripe female cone

M. macdonnellii – broken off fruits

Macrozamia macdonnellii (MacDonnell Ranges cycad)

Cupressaceae (cypress pine family)

There are about 13 species in Australia.

Genus *Callitris* (cypress pines)

Callitris glaucophylla (White cypress pine)

Of the Australian species of *Callitris*, *C. glaucophylla* is the most widespread, being found in all mainland States. It is a small resinous tree with small scented needle-like leaves which are whorled in threes along the stem.

The fruit is a globular woody cone about 2 cm wide. It opens by valves when it is mature, and a column can be seen inside the base. The seed has a semicircular wing. The wood of the species is of great commercial value because it is resistant to white ants and also to marine worms. The bark has a high tannin content and has been used commercially for tanning.

Callitris glaucophylla (White cypress pine)

ANGIOSPERMAE
(flowering plants)

There are 190 families of flowering plants found in the NT. About 95 of these can be found in CA-NT, and 57 families have been described here. As some selection was necessary it was decided to exclude grasses, rushes, sedges, and most pond weeds. Apart from this, emphasis has been placed on those plants most commonly seen. However, some species have been included because they are of particular interest. Some genera have been omitted. (The region described as CA-NT is that part of the NT between latitudes 20 degrees and 26 degrees – the SA border.)

Casuarinaceae (casuarina family)

The casuarina of CA-NT is *Allocasuarina decaisneana* (Desert oak) which is only found in the sand-dune areas west and south of Alice Springs. Its range is from the Great Sandy Desert of WA through to the Simpson Desert of CA. The name *casuarina* is derived from the Latin word *casuarius*, the name for the *cassowary* (the drooping branches resemble cassowary feathers). The prefix *allo* comes from Greek and means *different from*. Recently *Casuarina* has been divided into several groups and the CA casuarina is now *Allocasuarina*.

Casuarinas are trees or bushes with striated jointed branches. The leaves are reduced to scales and occur at joints in the drooping branchlets. There are separate male and female flowers. The winged seeds develop in woody cones.

Allocasuarina decaisneana (Desert oak)

Genus *Allocasuarina*

Allocasuarina decaisneana (Desert oak)

In the Desert oak there are 4 scale-leaves at each joint, the seed-cones are 2.5-10 cm long and the seeds 12-17 mm long. The flowers do not have petals. The female flowers are clustered together in short red cylindrical spikes formed by the clustered feathery stigmas. The male flowers are clustered in whorls on the ends of the branchlets. Desert oaks have hard wood, and the trunk is protected and insulated by the thick corky outer bark. The young trees look different: the seedling is a round spiky bundle of stems, which grows into a spiky young tree with numerous twig-like side branches. After many years, when the tree is quite tall, the broad branching canopy develops and the side branches drop off. Aborigines obtained water from pools trapped and protected inside the trunk.

Ulmaceae

Genus *Trema*

Trema aspera (Poison peach)

Poison peach can be found in rocky gorges such as Standley Chasm, Simpsons Gap and Ndahla Gorge. It is a shrubby bush with spreading branches, and leaves which look like those of a peach tree. The small black shiny fruits cluster at the leaf-angle. In dry periods many of the leaves drop, leaving the fruits on bare branches. This plant is considered poisonous to stock, but is not usually found where it is accessible to grazing.

Trema aspera (Poison peach)

Moraceae (fig family)

These grow as shrubs or trees, with milky sap and smooth bark. The flowers are inside the fig. Moraceae include *Morus* (the mulberry after which the family is named), *Ficus* (the fig), and *Artocarpus* (the breadfruit). There are about 800 species of fig world-wide; nearly 40 native to Australia. The India rubber plant, *Ficus elastica* and the garden fig *F. macrophylla* are introduced species.

Genus *Ficus* (figs)

Ficus platypoda (Native fig)

This is a many-stemmed sprawling shrub found in rocky gullies. It has smooth, shiny, dark-green leaves about 9 x 3 cm. The figs are globular, up to 1.2 cm in diameter, and turn from orange to red to purple as they ripen. Ripe fruits are juicy and sweet, and make very good eating. The flowers are inside the fig. They are fertilised by the larvae of a wasp which lays her eggs inside the fig. The fig is called a false fruit because it is really the fleshy swollen end of the stem.

Ficus platypoda (Native fig)

Right: *Ficus platypoda* – (Native fig). Diagrammatic representation of a section through the fig 'fruit', showing some of the tiny flowers. The true fruits are tiny nuts inside the fig, each about 1.5 mm long.
Below: Female flower (10 times normal size of 2 mm long) shows ovary surrounded by petals, and style and stigma.

Proteaceae (protea family)

The family name comes from the sea god Proteus who was said to be always changing his shape. It includes genera with many different forms; banksia and waratah are two. In CA-NT the family is represented by *Grevillea* and *Hakea*. World-wide there are about 1400 species in 75 genera, and in Australia about 750 species in 45 genera.

This is a family of shrubs and trees, which have bisexual flowers formed by 4 petal segments which are more or less united and tubular in the lower part. The seeds are in a dry follicle or a fleshy fruit.

Genera *Grevillea* and *Hakea*

In CA-NT *Grevillea* and *Hakea* are very similar. They both have flowers on short stalks in cylindrical bottle-brush-like clusters. Some clusters have up to 100 individual flowers. These flower clusters are very rich in honey and are much enjoyed as an Aboriginal food item. The leaves are very narrow, strap-like or terete (needle-like). The flower tube turns backwards in its upper part, and the globular end rests on one side of the tube. The stamens consist only of the anthers or pollen-sacs which are mounted on the petal segments. The style has a cone-shaped end (the pollen presenter) which holds the stigma. This is inserted into the flower at the end of the tube. When flowering occurs, the style becomes free, giving the flower clusters their familiar spider-like appearance. The fruit is a woody or leathery follicle. *Hakea* seeds have a wing on one side, and a woody seed-case with beaked end. *Grevillea* seeds have a hard round or oval seed-case which often has a projection or tail where the style used to be, and 2 round seeds which are sometimes wingless, but usually have a wing all around.

In CA-NT there are about 10 *Grevillea* species and about 10 hakeas.

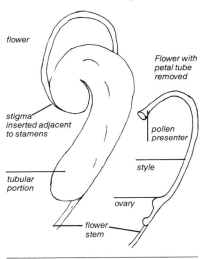

Grevillea and *Hakea* – flower shape

flower

Flower with petal tube removed

stigma inserted adjacent to stamens

pollen presenter

style

tubular portion

ovary

flower stem

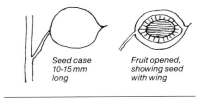

Grevillea fruits – *G. stenobotrya*

Seed case 10-15 mm long

Fruit opened, showing seed with wing

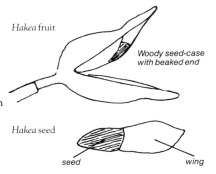

Hakea fruit

Woody seed-case with beaked end

Hakea seed

seed

wing

Genus *Grevillea*

Grevillea striata (Beefwood)

Beefwood, named for its red wood and sap, grows into a large tree. It has furrowed dark-brown bark. The leaves are strap-like and up to 30 cm long; flat, narrow, stiff and leathery, with longitudinal striations and a sharply pointed end. The cream flowers are in narrow cylindrical clusters 5-8 cm long. The seed is in an oval woody case with an upward-pointing tail.

The wood of Beefwood is hard and splits easily. For this reason it was used for roofing shingles, and is still used for fencing. A red resin oozes from the trunk and can also be obtained by heating the roots. This resin was used by the Aborigines as a glue, and also medicinally. The foliage is grazed by cattle and although palatable, it is not very nutritious. Beefwood is very tolerant of fire and drought, and survives by shooting from the roots. After good rains a crop of seedlings can often be seen. It is found scattered throughout the dry inland and is plentiful in flood out areas, such as the Ross River region.

Grevillea striata (Beefwood)

Grevillea striata (Beefwood) in flower

G. *stenobotrya* (Rattlepod grevillea)

Rattlepod grevillea grows in bushes or clumps, often on the crests of sand-dunes. The name *stenobotrya* means *narrow cluster*, and refers to the flower clusters which are 10-15 x 2-3 cm in size. These clusters are held erect, often in groups, and have hairless stalks.
The leaves are long and very narrow (up to 25 cm x 1-2 mm), and grooved underneath. The seed cases are round, flattened and tailed. They rattle together when dry. Like other desert grevilleas this one can shoot from the roots.

Grevillea stenobotrya (Rattlepod grevillea)

G. *eriostachya* (Honey grevillea)

Honey grevillea grows as a straggly spreading bush. The leaves are long, very narrow and grooved underneath. Long golden-green flower spikes extend laterally on spreading branches.
The flowers in the long spike open sequentially so that the end of the spike is in green bud, while on the basal part the golden flowers are fully open.
The flowers glisten with abundant nectar and the flower-stalks are densely hairy. The name *eriostachya* means *woolly spike*. The seed cases are also hairy. Honey grevillea can flower several times a year if there is rain. It shoots again from the roots after drought or fire.

Grevillea eriostachya (Honey grevillea)

G. *albiflora* (White spider flower)

The name *albiflora* means *white flowers*. White spider flower is a bush or small tree which grows on sand plains and dunes, and is found on Mt Ebenezer, Angus Downs and Curtin Springs. The white flowers are in cylindrical spikes which are longer and broader than those of Rattlepod grevillea, and they are on stronger stems. The spikes are held erect on finely-haired branches, and the stalks of the flower-spike are hairy. The divided leaves have long narrow lobes. The oval seed cases are covered by fine hairs. White spider flower shoots from the roots after fires.

Grevillea albiflora (White spider flower)

G. *juncifolia* (Desert grevillea)

Desert grevillea grows on sand plains and dunes, and is characterised by large orange flower clusters. The long narrow rush-like leaves are grooved and the stems striated (longitudinally striped). The stalks of the flower cluster are densely hairy and sticky, and the flower-surface is hairy. Nectar is abundant. The seed case is hard, round and flattened, with a hairy surface. This grevillea shoots again after fire.

Grevillea juncifolia (Desert grevillea)

G. *wickhamii* (Holly grevillea)

Holly grevillea is found on sand plains especially near rocky outcrops and gorges. The pale-green leaf has several sharply spiked lobes, giving it a shape like a holly leaf. The bright red flowers are in cylindrical clusters which hang down on drooping stems. The oval seed case is up to 2 cm long.

Grevillea wickhamii (Holly grevillea)

Genus *Hakea* (corkwoods)

Many hakeas are small gnarled trees, with a thick corky bark deeply cut into patterns. These trees are called corkwoods.

Hakea eyreana (Fork-leafed corkwood)

Fork-leafed corkwood is a small gnarled tree. Its corky bark is patterned like the tread of a large truck tyre. The wiry leaves are much-divided, with each leaf looking like many stems repeatedly forked and intertwined. Each stem-like lobe ends in a fork. The yellow flowers are clustered into oval-shaped spikes. The flower-stalks are hairy. The seed case is rounded and beaked, and the seeds are winged.

Flowers of *Hakea eyreana* (Fork-leafed corkwood)

Hakea eyreana (Fork-leafed corkwood)

H. suberea (Long-leafed corkwood)

This small gnarled tree has fissured corky bark. The long narrow leaves point upwards and out. They can be up to 30 cm long and 2-3 cm wide. The cream flowers are in untidy cylindrical clusters up to 12 cm long. The flower-stalks are hairy. The woody seed cases are rounded with a beaked end, and the seeds are winged. The name *suberea* means *corky*.

Hakea suberea (Long-leafed corkwood)

Flowers of *Hakea suberea* (Long-leafed corkwood)

H. leucoptera (Needlewood)

Needlewood is widespread in all mainland States. It grows as a many-stemmed shrub or small tree. The leaves are terete, and measure 3-9 cm x 1-2 mm. The leaves are smooth when mature and have scattered long hairs, and a sharp spine on the end. The creamy-white flowers are in hemispherical clusters 3-4 cm in diameter. The woody seed cases persist on the branches and are often seen at the next flowering.

They have a rounded base and beaked end. The seed has a white wing which is opaque. The name *leucoptera* means *white wing.*

Needlewood can shoot from the roots, and often spreads by suckering. It has water-bearing roots from which the Aborigines and explorers obtained water in time of need. These water-filled roots aid in the quick regeneration of the plant after fire.

Hakea leucoptera (Needlewood)

Santalaceae (sandalwood family)

These are shrubs or small trees which are semi-parasitic in that the seedling can only complete its development after a connection has been established between its roots and those of some other plant species. The flowers have a disc-like base. The fruit has a fleshy covering over a hard nut which encloses the seed.

Genus *Santalum*

This genus includes Quandong and Plum bush, and Australian sandalwood.

Santalum spicatum
(Australian sandalwood)

This is an important small tree of the dry inland of SA and WA, although it does not occur in NT. The strongly perfumed wood contains perfumed oil which is used for cabinet-making, carvings and incense. It was widely cut for export, especially to Asia, for both its wood and oil, but the industry has declined, because natural stands of trees have been cut out and not replaced, so that now Australian sandalwood is no longer economical to cut.

S. acuminatum (Quandong)

In CA-NT quandongs are only found to the south of Alice Springs. They are shrubs or trees up to 6 m high, and drooping in habit. The leaves are thick, grey-green and curved, and in opposite pairs. The species name *acuminatum* refers to the pointed leaves. The tiny flowers are in pyramid-shaped clusters. The flower is only 2-3 mm long with a red basal disc and 3 lobes to the cup. The round fruit is 2-3 cm in diameter. It consists of a hard, deeply pitted round stone (enclosing the seed) covered by a red fleshy layer which is edible. It was used by the Aborigines as a food, and is nowadays grown by home gardeners. The quandong flesh swells when soaked, and is very good for pies and jam. The nuts have many uses: Aborigines ate the kernel for its oil content, and used the nuts for decoration. Early settlers used to burn them as candles. They were also used at one stage as marbles for Chinese Checkers. The foliage is good grazing for stock, being both palatable and nutritious. Quandongs can be grown from the nut, and need to be planted near the roots of another plant; some gardeners use couch or honeysuckle, but it seems that other roots are satisfactory. In the natural state it is thought that spinifex may provide the host roots.

Santalum acuminatum (Quandong) – battered last fruit of old year with new flowers

Santalum acuminatum (Quandong)

S. *lanceolatum* (Plum bush)

Plum bush is a small tree about 2 m high. It is found throughout the NT and in adjacent States, and can be seen growing around the base of Ayers Rock. The thick drooping grey-green leaves are lanceolate in shape, in opposite pairs, and measure 3-8 x 2 cm. The flowers are small cream bells 6-8 mm long. The fleshy fruit is oval, 1 cm in diameter, and ripens to purple. It is edible. The foliage is palatable and nutritious topfeed for stock. The wood is like sandalwood, and was also exported for its perfumed wood and oil. This industry is not now economically viable.

Santalum lanceolatum (Plum bush)

Santalum lanceolatum (Plum bush)

Genus *Exocarpos*

Exocarpos sparteus (Slender cherry, Broom ballart)

Slender cherry is a much-branched shrub 2-3 m high, found in sand-dune and spinifex regions. The stems are longitudinally striped. The narrow leaves are only 5 mm long, triangular in cross-section, and drop early. The small flower has 5 or 6 jointed petal-like segments which do not drop, but enlarge to enclose the fruit. These flowers are in spikes 8-16 mm long. The small fruit has a swollen pink or red stalk (6-8 mm long) which can be eaten.

Exocarpos sparteus (Slender cherry, Broom ballart)

Genus *Anthobolus*

Anthobolus leptomerioides

This is a much-branched bright-green shrub up to 2 m high. The leaves are few, triangular in cross-section, and up to 1 cm long. The male and female flowers are on separate plants. The fruit is 5-8 mm long, on a stalk 10-12 mm long. It is green and turns orange.

Loranthaceae (mistletoe family)

Mistletoes are parasitic shrubs which are attached to a host tree from which they obtain water and nutrients. They usually attach to a branch by a wedge-shaped plug. In good seasons there can be a natural balance between mistletoes and host tree, but in times of drought or disease the host plant can die. Sometimes the mistletoe is the one to succumb. Mistletoe branches hang down, and break easily. The leaves are very variable. The flowers have 4-6 petals which form a tube. In some genera, for example *Amyema*, the floral tube is cut to its base and the petals are free. The fruit is a berry, with very sticky pulp surrounding a central seed. Fruits are spread by the birds that feed on them. In CA-NT the mistletoes are represented by 4 species of *Lysiana* and 9 species of *Amyema*. Two other family members, *Dendrophthos odontocalyx* and *Diplatia grandibractus*, are found north of Alice Springs.

Genus *Lysiana* (mistletoes)

In *Lysiana* the flower-tube is curved and remains undivided, and the flowers are either solitary or in clusters of 2. There are 4 species found in CA-NT.

Lysiana exocarpi (Harlequin mistletoe)

The name *exocarpi* means *outside fruit*, and refers to the outer fleshy covering of the seed. This mistletoe was given the common name 'harlequin' because of its red and green flowers. The curved flower-tube is red with yellow or green tips. The flowers are 2.5-5 cm long, and carried in clusters of 2 or 3 on a very short common stalk. The translucent fruits are red or black. The fruit is edible and was an Aboriginal food. The hairless leaves are narrow and curved, and 3-15 x 1 cm in size.

L. murrayi

This species has narrow flat leaves (3-6 cm x 1-3 mm). The flower is pink, yellow or white, with a winged stalk; the berry is red or pink.

L. spathulata

This species has flat leaves with blunt ends. The flowers are mostly red and in clusters of 2, and the berry is elliptic with a collar on its end.

Flower of *Lysiana exocarpi*

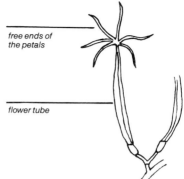

free ends of the petals

flower tube

L. subfalcata

In this species the leaves are flattened and clearly veined. The flowers are red or yellow, in clusters of 2 on a short common stalk. The pear-shaped fruit is yellow.

Lysiana exocarpi (Harlequin mistletoe) berries

Lysiana exocarpi (Harlequin mistletoe) flowers

Genus *Amyema* (mistletoes)

In *Amyema* the petals are divided right down to the base of the flower. The flowers are in several clusters of 3. There are 9 species of *Amyema* found in CA-NT.

Amyema preissii

This hairless shrub has needle-like leaves 2-8 cm x 1-2 mm. The flowers are in 2 or 3 clusters of 3. They are red, 2-2.5 cm long, with the separate petals curving backwards. The round berries are pink, white or red. This mistletoe is widespread, especially on acacias.

Flower of *Amyema preissii* (mistletoe)

Amyema preissii – flowers

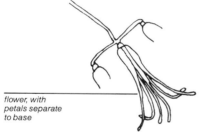

flower, with
petals separate
to base

Amyema preissii – berries

A. gibberulum

This is a hairy needle-leaf mistletoe.
The grey terete leaves are 5-10 cm long
and resemble those of needlewood, and
some other grevilleas and hakeas on
which it is found. The flowers are in
2 clusters of 3. The red flower is 3-5 cm
long and the petals are free. The whole
plant has a hairy covering.

Amyema gibberulum – flowers

A. maidenii

Maiden's mistletoe has wide, pale green
leaves 2-6 cm long. They are flat and
rounded, and wider at the distal end.
The plant has a dense covering of fine
white or brown hairs. The green flowers
are in clusters of 2 groups of 3. They are
densely hairy and are cut right to the
base. The hairy yellow berry has a small
crown at the top. This mistletoe is
common on mulga, dead finish and
acacia bush.

Amyema maidenii – flowers

A. miquelii

This is frequently found on eucalypts.
The leaves often look a coppery colour.
They are mostly hairless, and are long
(4-28 cm). The red flowers are stalked,
and in clusters of 3. The pear-shaped
fruit is 8-12 mm long.

Amyema miquelii – flowers

Polygonaceae (dock family)

Docks grow as herbs and shrubs.
They have a membranous sheath around
the base of the leaf. The small flower has
5 or 6 joined petal-like segments which
do not drop, but enlarge to enclose the
fruit. Many species are successful weeds,
often found in disturbed ground.
In CA-NT there are both native and
introduced species.

Genus *Polygonum*

This is the genus after which the family
is named. The name *polygonum* comes
from Greek and means *many knees*
(referring to the many nodes of the
stems). Species of *Polygonum* have small
flowers in the leaf-stem angle, a sheath
around the leaf-base, and a woody nut as
the fruit. In CA-NT there are 3 native
and 1 introduced species.

Genus *Rumex* (docks and sorrels)

Docks and sorrels are the best known of
this family. The name *rumex* comes from
the Latin word for *sorrel*. Wild sorrels
native to Europe have been used as herbs
for centuries. Sorrels and docks have
also been used medicinally. All *Rumex*
species are edible, and the leaves may be
cooked as a vegetable. The small flowers
are in long clusters and these develop
into winged fruits, each enclosing a nut.

Rumex vesicarius (Rosy dock, Ruby dock,
Native hops, Wild hops)

This fleshy-leafed annual can be seen
spread over the countryside after good
winter rains. The red fruits have 3 wings
and look rather like hops. Although
often called Native hops, the plant is
neither native nor hops. The fruits of
this dock are inflated. The name
vesicarius comes from a Latin word *vesica*
meaning a *sac* or *bladder*. Rosy dock was

introduced last century, supposedly in
the stuffing of camel saddles. It is native
to northern Africa and western Asia.

Rumex vesicarius (Rosy dock, Ruby dock,
Native hops, Wild hops)

R. brownii and *R. crystallinus*

These are weedy plants which have dry
winged fruits. The plants are not fleshy,
and the fruits are not inflated. They
are native to CA-NT. The seed of
R. crystallinus is one the Aborigines
used for cakes.

Genus *Emex*

Emex australis (Three-cornered Jack)

This is an introduced weed with 3 long
hard spines on the fruit. It has been
suspected as a sheep poison, but is not a
problem where cattle are run.

Genus *Muehlenbeckia*

Muehlenbeckia cunninghamii (lignum)

Lignum is a many-stemmed, much branched spiny shrub which usually drops its leaves as it matures. It grows in swampy areas and can be seen on the edge of claypans. The small flowers are in small clusters. The fruit is a shiny nut 5 mm long.

Gyrostemonaceae (Gyrostemon family)

Gyrostemons grow as bushes or small trees which are hairless, and they have small flowers less than 5 mm in diameter. Male and female flowers are separate, and may be on the same or separate trees. The family occurs only in Australia.

Genus *Codonocarpus*

Codonocarpus cotinifolius (Desert poplar)

The name *codonocarpus* means *bell-shaped fruit*. Desert poplar is widespread in dry inland Australia. In its shape and leaf it looks very like the European poplar. The hairless broad green leaves are 2-6 cm long with a pointed or rounded end. The male and female flowers are on separate trees; they look very similar, but the male flower has a short stalk and the female flower-stalk is over 1 cm long. The fruits are bell-shaped, 1-1.5 cm long, with many fruitlets. The trees are short-lived; they grow rapidly, especially after fire, and last only about six years.

Muehlenbeckia cunninghamii (lignum)

Codonocarpus cotinifolius
(Desert Poplar)

male flowers

fruit

Codonocarpus cotinifolius (Desert poplar)

Genus *Gyrostemon*

Gyrostemon ramulosus
(Camel poison bush)

Gyrostemon ramulosus is found in sand-dune and spinifex areas. It has been called Camel poison bush because several explorers, including Giles, had camels die after eating the bushes; however, some other quite different species are also called Camel poison. The name *ramulosus* means *much-branched* or *twiggy*. *G. ramulosus* grows as a bush or tree up to 3 m high. It is much-branched and has grey corky bark. The dark-green leaves are long and very narrow (2-6 cm x 1 mm). The wheel-like flowers are small, with male and female flowers on separate bushes. The pear-shaped fruit is about 8 mm long and has many fruitlets.

Gyrostemon ramulosis (Camel poison bush)

Gyrostemon ramulosis (Camel poison bush) fruit

G. tepperi (Double-seeded emu bush)

This small, much-branched shrub is found amongst the mulga and spinifex and grows to 1.5 m. The leaves are long and very narrow (1-5 cm x 1 mm).

The seed capsule has 2 compartments. This species was one of those used by the Aborigines to poison water-holes – by leaving a branch lying in the water – in order to stupefy game.

Nyctaginaceae

Most members of this family are native to the American tropics. They include bougainvillea. The characteristics of the family are: opposite leaves, flower with cup and petals joined, and fruit (with sticky ribs and glands) enclosed in the persisting flower-cup.

Genus *Boerhavia*

Boerhavia coccinea (Tar vine)

There are several species of *Boerhavia* in CA-NT and they are not easily distinguished. The most common is *B. coccinea*. Tar vine is a small prostrate vine-like perennial with a strong taproot. It is often found in disturbed ground, and is noticed because of its stickiness; the twining stems are so sticky it is reported that the Aborigines used it to make snares for small birds and animals. They also baked the taproot as a vegetable. The small flowers are pink or lilac and usually in small clusters. The fruit (2-3.5 mm long) is sticky, hairy and ribbed.

Boerhavia coccinea (Tar vine)

Aizoaceae (pigface family)

This family includes pigface, hogweed and carpetweed. Aizoaceae are succulent, often prostrate shrubs which are usually perennials. The fleshy or succulent leaves may be opposite or in whorls, but can be alternate. Some have sheathing at the leaf-base. The small insignificant flower is a lobed cup without normal petals. Those species of pigface which appear to have long narrow petals have really got petal-like stamens. The fruit is usually a capsule. There are 12 species found in CA-NT.

Genus *Gunniopsis*

G. quadrifida (Sturt's pigface)

The name *quadrifida* means *divided into 4 parts*, and refers to the 4 segments of the flower. The plant is succulent, whitish-grey, with paired terete leaves. The flowers have white pointed lobes. The capsule is top-shaped with a depressed end. The plant grows up to 40 cm high.

Gunniopsis zygophylloides (Twin-leaf pigface)

Gunniopsis zygophylloides (Twin-leaf pigface)

This small prostrate green shrub is also called *Aizoon zygophylloides*. The succulent leaves are flat, 1-2.5 cm long, and covered with small blisters. The flowers are 8 mm long and have 4 fleshy yellow lobes. The fruit is a globular capsule.

Genus *Trianthema*

Trianthema triquetra (Red spinach)

This small prostrate annual has opposite sheathed succulent leaves which are narrow, and 1-2 cm long. The small flower has a 5 lobed cup with a glistening red disc. The flowers are in groups of 1-3. The name *trianthema* comes from the Greek for *three flowers*. The succulent stems are often reddish. The fruit is a

very small capsule with a flattened end. This plant is widespread in moist areas, and in disturbed ground.

T. pilosa and *T. oxycalyptra* are also found in CA-NT.

Trianthema trinquetra (Red spinach)

Genus *Zaleya*

Zaleya galericulata (Hogweed)

This widespread red-stemmed perennial shoots readily after rain. The leaves are thick, hairless and oblong, with a sheathed base. The fruit is a capsule. Like all perennials, Hogweed is valuable as a soil stabiliser.

Portulacaceae (pigweed family)

This family of succulent plants includes pigweeds and parakeelyas. The flowers have 2 sepals and 4-8 petals which may be large and brightly coloured. The fruit is a capsule that usually contains many small seeds which are often kidney-shaped.

Genus *Portulaca* (pigweed)

Pigweeds are widespread throughout the world, with 15 species in Australia. They are prostrate succulents often with tuberous roots. The leaves are spirally arranged and the flowers have no stalks. The capsule, which opens at the top, is a small cup enclosing numerous tiny seeds.

Portulaca oleracea (Munyeroo)

Munyeroo is widespread throughout the world, and is called Purslane in Europe. It looks very like *P. intraterranea*. It is found in moist areas and disturbed ground. For centuries it has been used medicinally, and as a vegetable. The Aborigines used it extensively, grinding the nutritious seed to make cakes. They needed to pull up the plants from a large area, and leave them to dry, in order to collect the seed to make flour. Explorers, pioneers and Aborigines used Munyeroo as a vegetable – raw and cooked – and relied on its effectiveness against scurvy. The small succulent has a strong taproot which was also eaten by the Aborigines.

Zaleya galericulata (Hogweed)

Both taproot and fleshy leaves are still eaten when available. The stems are reddish-brown and the leaves are opposite. The flowers are small, 4-5 mm long, and without stalks. The small capsules contain many tiny black comma-shaped seeds. This plant is widespread, especially after rain.

P. intraterranea (Buttercup pigface)

This is a small succulent, very like Munyeroo. The yellow flowers are larger, 14-17 mm long, and have short stalks. The leaves are alternate and the stems are thick and reddish. Like Munyeroo, the taproot, leaves and seed were important Aboriginal foods. The comma-shaped seeds are slightly different from Munyeroo. Buttercup pigface is found in sand-dune regions.
(see photo overleaf)

Portulaca intraterranea (Buttercup pigface)

P. pilosa (Hairy pigface)

This small succulent has terete leaves, and yellow flowers in clusters surrounded by long hairs. The capsule has many small black seeds. The Aborigines used the down from around the flowers for ceremonial decoration.

Genus *Calandrinia* (parakeelyas)

There are about 150 species of parakeelya found in Australia and America, 11 or more of these in CA-NT. Some are sufficiently different as to be easily distinguished, but others are very alike. The differences are in seed and seed-capsule, flower-parts, leaves, and the direction of the fruiting stalk. All parakeelyas were used as a vegetable by both the Aborigines and the early settlers. Parakeelyas are small succulent plants with a taproot, a short stem and leaves mainly at the base. The flower has 4-11 petals, often 5, and may be pink, purple or white. Stamens may be few or many. The style has 3 or 4 stigmas. The fruiting capsule opens with 3 or 4 valves, or with 1 pore at the top. The small seeds are usually numerous, and smooth or patterned.

Calandrinia balonensis (Broad-leaf parakeelya)

Broad-leaf parakeelya has 5 notched purple petals about 1.5 cm long, many stamens, and 3 stigma branches with a short style. The flat, fleshy leaves have a vein on the surface. Leaves occur on the flower-stem as well as at the base. The small egg-shaped capsule hangs down from the stem, and the small kidney-shaped seeds are black or dark-red, with a knobbly surface.

Calandrinia balonensis (Broad-leaf parakeelya) flower

C. reticulata (a parakeelya)

This species has a leafless flower-stalk, and the fruiting stalk is erect. The stamens are numerous and there are 3 stigmas.

C. remota (a parakeelya)

This species has leaves mainly at the base. They are flattened and grooved underneath. The fruit stalk hangs down. The petals are about 1.5 cm long. The stamens are numerous and there are 3 stigmas. The red-brown seeds are smooth and glossy.

C. polyandra (a parakeelya)

This species has many large leaves at the base. The petals are not notched. The stamens are numerous and there are 3 stigmas. The fruiting stalk hangs down. The name *polyandra* means *many stamens*.

C. pumila (Tiny purslane)

This tiny, delicate plant may have green or pink fleshy stems and leaves. The leaves are only at the base, and they are stalked and spade-like. The small flowers are only up to 3 mm long on stalks 2-10 cm long. The stamens are few and there are 3 stigmas. The fruiting stalk is erect. Tiny purslane is found north of Alice Springs.

C. eremaea (Small purslane)

In Small purslane the leaves are at the base. They are terete and without stalks. The flowers, with 5 slightly notched petals, are small and on long stalks. They have many stamens and 3 stigmas. The fruit-capsule hangs down.

C. disperma (a parakeelya)

This plant has only a few leaves which are narrow-oblong, 2-5 cm long, and mostly basal. The orange-pink flowers have 4 stamens and 3 stigmas. The fruit-stalk is erect. The capsule is swollen at the base and the 2 pear-shaped seeds emerge from a pore in the top. The name *disperma* means *two seeds*.

Calandrinia remota (a parakeelya)

Calandrinia pumila (Tiny purslane)

C. lehmannii (a parakeelya)

This has basal spade-like leaves. The flowers have 5 spade-like petals, numerous stamens and 3 stigmas. The capsule is ovoid.

C. stagnensis (a parakeelya)

This has only a few leaves which are straight and narrow. The flowers have 5-6 pink petals, 8-11 stamens and 4 stigmas.

C. pleiopetala (a parakeelya)

This species has many narrow oblong leaves without stalks. The flowers have 8 petals. The name *pleiopetala* means *more petals.* The fruits are on spreading stems. The stamens are numerous, and there are 4 stigmas.

C. ptychosperma (Creeping parakeelya)

The stems are pink to brown, and the leaves numerous and without stalks. The flower has 4-7 pointed petals which are pink-purple, 5-9 stamens and 4-5 stigmas. The name *ptychosperma* means *folded seed.* The seeds are ribbed. The fruits are on spreading stalks.

Calandrinia ptychosperma (Creeping parakeelya)

Calandrinia stagnensis

42

Chenopodiaceae (saltbush family)

This family includes saltbush, bluebush, goosefoot, pricklebush and samphire. It has over 100 genera worldwide, several found only in Australia. There are 15 genera in CA-NT, and many species. Saltbush survives and thrives in poor, salty soil, and in arid regions. Most species are palatable to stock and as saltbush, bluebush and pricklebush are especially prevalent in salty country, they contribute to the grazing potential of vast areas of Australia. The plant-tissue often tastes salty. Some may be used as vegetables once the salt has been boiled out. The plant surface may be covered with a fine floury powder, and may also be scaly or haired (though some are hairless). Leaves are usually present, but are absent in samphires. The flowers are small and often the two sexes may be in separate flowers, sometimes on separate plants. There are no petals in the usual sense. The fruit may be dry, or a berry, and is surrounded by the hardened flower-segments. Each genus has a typical fruit.

Halosarcia sp.

The leafless group

Samphires are leafless plants with fleshy jointed branches.

Genus *Halosarcia*

In *Halosarcia* the flowers are buried in fleshy segments which are soft and fertile during the first year. Later these harden to form permanent branches and stems. The segments become coloured and translucent and the plant is often called Beadbush. There are 6 species of *Halosarcia* in CA-NT, and these can be identified by their seeds and fruits. They are found mainly in salt-lakes and near salty claypans.

Halosarcia sp.

Genus *Tecticornia*

Tecticornia verrucosa

This succulent plant is like *Halosarcia* but the fleshy flowering spikes extend sideways from the stem. Some species of *Sclerostegia* and *Pachycornia* are also found in salty places in CA-NT.

The narrow-leafed group

These have narrow leaves which are hairless, or have silky hairs. They include genera with 3 different types of fruit: a berry, a spiny fruit, and a winged fruit.

Enchylaena has a berry, *Sclerolaena* has a spiny fruit, and *Maireana, Salsola* and *Babbagia* have winged fruits.

Genus *Enchylaena*

Enchylaena tomentosa (Ruby saltbush)

The name *enchylaena* is derived from a Greek word and means *succulent cloak,* referring to the berry. The word *tomentosa* means *covered with hair.* There is just one

Tecticornia verrucosa

species in the genus. The terete leaves are succulent. There is a fine downy covering on the leaves and the stems, which are striated. The tiny flowers are not easily seen, but the fleshy red fruits draw attention to Ruby saltbush. This fruit is edible and tasty, and was a food item for the Aborigines.

Enchylaena tomentosa (Ruby saltbush)

Genus *Sclerolaena* – also called *Bassia* (prickle bushes)

These are shrubby plants with narrow leaves which are often silky-haired. The fruit is a large hard prickle with 2-6 spines. Each species has a prickle with individual shape and character. *Sclerolaena* is only found in Australia. There are 28 species in CA-NT.

S. bicornis (Goathead burr)

This much-branched shrub grows to 60 cm high, and is densely hairy. The fruiting-prickle is tightly enveloped in white wool. It has 2 long rigid spines which diverge.

Saltbush family – prickle bushes
Sclerolaena species fruits

Sclerolaena bicornis   *Sclerolaena crenata*
(Goathead burr)

S. birchii (Galvanised burr)

This much-branched small shrub is grey due to a dense hairy covering. The fruiting-prickle has 4-5 spreading spines, 2 being larger.

Sclerolaena bicornis (Goathead burr)

Sclerolaena birchii (Galvanised burr)

S. eriacantha (Silky copper burr)

This is a small shrub about 30 cm high with spreading hairy branches.
The fruiting-prickle is almost hidden beneath silky hairs. It has 2 long spines which diverge.

Sclerolaena eriacantha (Silky copper burr)

S. crenata

This small prickle bush grows up to 25 cm high, and is found to the north of Alice Springs. The fruit is hairless and ribbed and has 2 divergent spines.

There are many other prickle bushes found in CA-NT.

Sclerolaena crenata (prickle bush)

Genus *Maireana* (bluebushes)
– also called *Kochia*

Bluebushes have narrow leaves and winged fruits. They are valuable fodder plants in dry areas.

There are 27 species of *Maireana* in CA-NT. A fruit is essential for identification.

Maireana campanulata (Bluebush)

The name *campanulata* means *bell-shaped.* This plant has a bell-shaped fruit, with a narrow horizontal wing which has no slit. The branches are hairy, and the narrow leaves are succulent and hairless.

Maireana campanulata (Bluebush)

Bluebush fruits, showing wings

M. *georgei* (Satiny bluebush)

Satiny bluebush is a small shrub with woolly branches and narrow leaves which may be silky. The fruit is shaped like a spinning-top, with a horizontal wing which has one slit.

M. campanulata

M. *georgei*

Maireana georgei (Satiny bluebush)

Genus *Salsola*

Salsola kali (Roly-poly, Buckbush, Tumbleweed)

The name *salsola* comes from the Latin word *salsus* meaning *salted,* and refers to the plant's ability to grow in salty ground. Roly-poly is a small, stiff, round prickle-bush 30 cm-1 m tall. It is often seen, after it has dried and broken off, rolling across the countryside.
The prickles are not on the fruits, but on the ends of the stiff narrow leaves. The fruit is 4-7 mm wide, with a horizontal rounded wing which has 5 segments. The species is widespread in Australia, and also found in the temperate parts of Europe and America. The Aborigines obtained an edible grub from the root.

Salsola kali (Roly-poly, Buckbush, Tumbleweed)

The wide flat-leafed group

The genera of this group may have a berry or a dry fruit. Included are: *Einadia* and *Rhagodia* which have a berry, *Atriplex* which has a dry fruit with 2 bracts, and *Dysphania* which has a dry fruit with 1-4 segments.

Genus *Einadia*

Einadia nutans (Climbing saltbush)

The word *nutans* means *nodding,* and refers to the drooping branches of this climbing perennial. The leaves are usually lobed at the base, and the fruit is a red berry. The plant is widespread and palatable to stock. This is the only *Einadia* found in CA-NT.

Einadia nutans (Climbing saltbush)

Genus *Rhagodia*

Rhagodias are found only in Australia.
They are small shrubs and scramblers
with leaves which are usually wide and
flat, often with a floury covering.
The fruit is a berry.

There are 3 *Rhagodia* species found
in CA-NT.

Rhagodia spinescens (Thorny saltbush)

This shrub grows to 1.5 m high, and has
spiny branches. The leaves, 1-2 cm long,
are oblong or oval with a slender stalk,
and have a floury covering. The fruit is
a red berry. The foliage is palatable and
is a useful stockfeed because it is fairly
widespread.

Rhagodia spinescens (Thorny saltbush)

Genus *Atriplex* (saltbush)

Saltbush has separate male and female
flowers which are in clusters. The female
flowers have no petals, but 2 bracts which
are fused around the seed. They may have
wings. The leaves are flat, and the plants
have a floury or scaly covering. There
are 23 species found in CA-NT.

Atriplex nummularia (Old man saltbush)

Atriplex nummularia (Old man saltbush)

Old man saltbush is probably the best known saltbush in CA-NT. It is a large, untidy blue-grey bush 2-3 m high. The leaves are wide, flat, scaly and floury. It is found in the Alice Springs region, south to the Flinders Ranges, and in the eastern States. These big bushes can be seen in the parks and wastelands of Alice Springs, especially in the coolibah swamp near the eastside connector-road. The leaves are stalked, circular to ovate. Male and female flowers are on separate bushes. After a small amount of rain the bushes flower. The pollen is spread by the wind, and after fertilisation the leafy bracts of the female flower grow large and thick, surrounding the developing seed in a fan-shaped fruit.

Old man saltbush is a perennial. It is the largest of the Australian saltbushes and is found especially in low-lying salty, swampy places. It is a valuable stock food, and survives well in times of drought because of its extensive root system. However, it is vulnerable to over-stocking and has been eaten out in places.

A. vesicaria (Bladder saltbush)

Bladder saltbush grows 30-70 cm high. The oblong grey-green leaves have a whitish surface and a short stalk. Male and female flowers are on separate bushes. The fruit is bladder-like. This long-lived perennial is widespread in dry salty areas and provides good forage in periods of drought. It also has great value in binding the soil. Overgrazing can destroy it. The name *vesicaria* comes from the Latin word *vesica* meaning *sac* or *bladder*.

Saltbush fruit – *Atriplex nummularia*

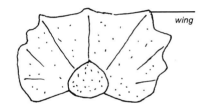

Atriplex nummularia (Old man saltbush) – female non-fruiting branch; note leaves.

A. *holocarpa* (Pop saltbush)

Pop saltbush grows in small round bushes about 30 cm high. The male and female flowers are on the same bush. The fruit is a spongy round ball 6-12 mm long.

There are other genera of the saltbush family found in CA-NT.

Atriplex holocarpa (Pop saltbush)

Genus *Dysphania* (crumbweeds)

There are 7 species of crumbweed in CA-NT. Many of them have basal leaves and flowering spikes reaching upwards. Others have their small flowers in clusters. The genus name *Dysphania* comes from the Greek *dysphanos* meaning *hardly visible,* referring to the very small flowers. Crumbweeds are annuals.

Dysphania rhadinostachya (Rat tails)

Rat tails have basal elliptic leaves 1-2 cm long with undulating edges. The flower spikes rise erect to about 30 cm, like green rat-tails.

Dysphania rhadinostachya (Rat tails)

Amaranthaceae (pussytail family)

Genus *Ptilotus* (pussytails)

We call *Ptilotus* species 'pussytails' because of their distinctive flower heads. The flowers are gathered closely together to form the fluffy heads, which resemble pussy tails. Each flower consists of 5 long, narrow, stiff, fluffy tepals. The flower, which has no stalk, is covered on the outside with long fluffy hairs, and enclosed at the base by a bract and 2 bracteoles. The seed develops inside the closed tepals which act as a seed case, and is distributed by the wind.

There are altogether 23 pussytails found in CA-NT. They vary in the following ways: their leaves and stems, the hairy covering, the colour, shape and size of the pussytail, and in the details of the flower.

In CA-NT there are also several species of *Amaranthus* and *Alternanthera* which belong to this family.

Ptilotus atriplicifolius (Crimson foxtail) flower

P. atriplicifolius (Crimson foxtail)

This perennial pussytail is found in all mainland States. The flower heads are cylindrical or globular, about 5 x 3 cm, and pink. The tepals are silvery with crimson tips and long grey and white hairs. The inner tepals are bearded. The stamens are crimson. The leaves are pale grey-green due to a dense covering of star-shaped hairs. They are about 5 x 4 cm and have a wavy margin. There are several varieties of this species.

Ptilotus atriplicifolius (Crimson foxtail)

P. obovatus (Silvertails)

Silvertails is a perennial, and is very like Crimson foxtail. The flower spikes are 1-3 cm long, and hemispherical or cylindrical. The flower stems may be bent at right-angles. There are several varieties.

P. helipteroides (Hairy mulla mulla)

Hairy mulla mulla has a deep pink to lilac pussytail, about 3 x 2 cm, with a white tuft at the top. It is an ephemeral herb which appears after rain.

Ptilotus obovatus (Silvertails) flowers

Ptilotus helipteroides (Hairy mulla mulla)

Ptilotus helipteroides (Hairy mulla mulla)

P. exaltatus (Tall mulla mulla)

The name *exaltatus* means *tall*. The bush is a perennial which grows to 1.5 m. The leaves are large and fleshy, up to 20 x 7 cm. The flower heads are deep pink and up to 20 x 4.5 cm. The flowers are covered with long silky hairs, and the stamens are crimson. There are several varieties.

Ptilotus exaltatus (Pink mulla mulla)

Ptilotus exaltatus (Pink mulla mulla)

P. nobilis (Yellowtails)

Like Tall mulla mulla, Yellowtails has long flower heads, up to 22 cm long and 4-5 cm wide. These cylindrical heads are yellow-green. The flowers have a strong perfume and feathery yellowish hairs. The plant is a perennial with a deep root system. The leaves are hairless, fleshy and spade-shaped.

Ptilotus nobilis (Yellowtails)

P. macrocephalus (Large green pussytail)

The name *macrocephalus* means *large head*, and *P. macrocephalus* is distinguished by having heads at least 5 cm wide. They are not as long as those of Yellowtails, but are up to 12 cm long. The flowers are pale-green and hairy. The stamens are yellow. The plant is a perennial, up to 1 m tall, and has stems that are either single or branching. The leaves are narrow.

Ptilotus macrocephalus (Large green pussytail)

Ptilotus macrocephalus (Large green pussytail)

P. polystachyus (Longtails)

This has long narrow pale-green pussytails, 4-15 x 2-3 cm in size. The flowers are scented, yellow-green and hairy. There is a red-brown form which is called Red pussytail. The plant is a perennial up to 1 m high, with erect stems. The leaves are narrow and wavy, about 10 cm long. There are several varieties.

Ptilotus polystachyus (Longtails)

P. latifolius (Tangled mulla mulla)

Tangled mulla mulla is an annual which grows on sand-dunes. The small round bushes present a tangled mass of white woolly stems. The silvery-white flower heads are almost globular, and the leaves are wide.

Dilleniaceae

These are shrubs with bright yellow flowers.

Genus *Hibbertia* (guinea flowers)

Hibbertia glaberrima (Guinea flower)

This Guinea flower grows in the rocky gorges of the central mountains of CA-NT. The shrubs grow to 50 cm tall. The plant is hairless with woody stems and green shiny leaves. The flowers are vivid yellow, 2-3 cm in diameter, with 5 rounded petals which overlap and have crinkly edges. The fruit is a capsule.

Droseraceae (sundew family)

In this family the plants kill insects and absorb the nutrients, using glandular secretions from the tentacle-like hairs on the leaves.

Hibbertia glaberrima (Guinea flower)

Genus *Drosera* (sundews)

There are 2 sundews in CA-NT.

Drosera indica (Sundew)

The name *drosera* is derived from the Greek word *droseros* meaning *dewy*, and refers to the glandular hairs. This species has long thread-like leaves with a surface covering of sticky tentacle-like hairs 4 mm long. The white or lilac flowers are on a long stem.

D. burmannii (Sundew)

This species has leaves in a basal rosette 2-5 cm across. The leaves are wedge-shaped, about 2 x 1 cm in size, and are green turning red. The white flowers are on a long stem.

Drosera indica (Sundew)

Capparaceae (caper family)

Genus *Capparis*

Capparis spinosa ssp. *nummularia*
(Wild passionfruit)

Wild passionfruit is not related to
passionfruit but is a member of the caper
family. (Capers are the pickled buds of
a Mediterranean variety of *C. spinosa*).
Wild passionfruit grows as sprawling
prickly bushes up to 1 m tall. The leathery
leaves are oval, with pointed ends, a
hooked tip and 2 spines at the base.
The large white flowers are on long
stalks. They have 4 white petals, 4 sepals
and numerous long white stamens.
A central stalk which protrudes above
the stamens has the ovary on its tip.
This grows to become a smooth oval
fruit about 4 cm long, with yellow pith
and large black seeds. Wild passionfruit
is found near rocky hills and riverbeds,
and is widespread in the regions of
Ross River and Trephina Gorge. It is
edible, and was used by the Aborigines.

Capparis spinosa ssp. *nummularia*
(Wild passionfruit)

Capparis spinosa ssp. *nummalaria* (Wild passionfruit)

C. mitchellii (Wild orange)

This small tree is scattered throughout CA-NT and the dry parts of Queensland, NSW and SA. It starts as a prickly branching shrub which develops into a small tree with a dense canopy. The dense canopy makes it look a bit like an orange tree, but it is not related. The oval leathery leaves have pointed ends, and a grey-green appearance which is due to the hairy covering. The large pale yellow flowers have cupped hairy sepals. The flower is on a stem 3-4 cm long, has fringed petals 3 cm long, and many stamens 4 cm long. The fruit grows in the centre of the flower on a stalk 5 cm long. It is globular and hairy, black when ripe, and edible.

The foliage is extensively grazed and new growth is slow. The species is tolerant to fire.

C. umbonata (Northern wild orange)

This small tree is much like Wild orange, but the fruit is hairless, and the hairless drooping leaves are long and narrow – about 20 x 2 cm. Young shoots have smaller prickly leaves, about 4 cm long. Northern wild orange is found in the NT north from Barrow Creek, and in the Gibson Desert in WA. It is drought resistant, and moderately palatable to stock.

Two other species of *Capparis* are found to the north of Alice Springs.

Capparis mitchellii (Wild orange)

Genus *Cleome*

Cleome viscosa (Tickweed)

Cleome is another genus of the caper family. Tickweed or *Cleome viscosa* is a small yellow-flowered plant found in sandy places, often by roadsides. It typically grows 20-30 cm tall. The name *viscosa* refers to the covering of glandular hairs which make the plant quite sticky to touch. The yellow flowers have 4 petals, and the leaves have 3-5 lobes. The seeds are in a long narrow cylindrical pod which has a knob at its tip. *Cleome viscosa* is used medicinally by the Aborigines in Australia, and also by people in Asia; as a dressing for wounds, packs for headaches, juices for ear-ache and internally, for worms.

Cleome viscosa (Tickweed)

Brassicaceae (cabbage family)
– also called Cruciferae

Brassicaceae or Cruciferae is the cabbage family. It includes all the cabbage and turnip species; cresses, mustards, peppercress and radish, and also the garden ornamentals alyssum, wallflower and stock. In CA-NT quite a large number of species from this family grow wild, including both introduced weeds and native plants. The particular feature of the family is that the flower has four petals arranged in a cross-like shape, the word *cruciferae* means *bearing a cross*. There are also four sepals, and usually six stamens. The seed-capsules may be long, narrow and cylindrical, or short, broad and purse-like. All have two compartments separated by a partition.

There are several native and introduced cresses in CA-NT including Ward's weed, various pepper-cresses, Shepherd's purse, Thread-petals and introduced wild mustards.

Most of the cresses and cabbage family are edible and the Aborigines used several species as steamed vegetables, by crushing them between hot rocks.

The name Brassicaceae comes from the Latin word for *cabbage.*

Altogether in CA-NT there are 24 species in 11 genera.

Brassica tournefortii (Turnip weed)

This is a widespread annual which has been introduced from the Mediterranean region. It is found in sandy soils and in disturbed places. The deeply lobed leaves are mainly at the base of the plant. The small flowers are pale yellow, 5-8 mm long. The seed-capsule is a long, narrow, cylindrical pod 3-7 cm x 2 mm, with a beaked end.

This weed is not palatable to stock and can therefore be a pest when it crowds out native pasture. The dry stems and pods tend to remain after seeding, and are rough and troublesome to walk through.

Genus *Blennodia*

Blennodia canescens (Wild stock)

In some years of good winter rains, masses of yellow and white daisies are mixed with sweet-smelling white flowers. These flowers look like 'single' stocks, and are members of the cabbage and stock family.

Wild stock is an annual which grows about 20-30 cm tall. The flowers are four-petalled and usually white, but may be pink or lilac. They are on upright stems in clusters on erect spreading stalks. The seed-capsule is a narrow cylindrical pod with a beaked end. It spreads out and upwards from each stem.

B. pterosperma (Wild stock)

This is another wild stock which also occurs in CA-NT. It is very similar to *B. canescens:* the main difference is that the seed pods spread out downwards.

Blennodia canescens (Wild stock)

Pittosporaceae (pittosporum family)

Genus *Pittosporum*

There are many pittosporums native to Australia. The name *pittosporum* is derived from the Greek words *pitta* meaning *pitch* and *sporos* meaning *seed,* because of the sticky pulp surrounding the seeds.

Pittosporum phylliraeoides
(Weeping pittosporum)

This tree is widespread throughout the dry inland, as well as in more temperate climates. *Phylliraeoides* (a mis-spelling of *phillyreoides*) was named because of its likeness to a plant called *Phillyrea* – the ending, *oides,* means *like.* Weeping pittosporum is a small tree with drooping branches. The pointed leaves are straight and narrow, 10 x 1 cm, and hairless.

The flowers are small cream bells which hang on stalks in the leaf/stem angle. During dry periods many leaves are shed, leaving only clusters at the end of branches. When leaves are missing the flower stalks seem to emerge directly from the branch. The round pale-orange seed capsules look like apricots, but are hard. They split open to show the seeds enveloped in sticky red pulp. The seeds are very bitter, but are much enjoyed by birds and are spread in this way.

The foliage is a very nutritious and palatable stock fodder. The tree also has a reputation as a medicinal plant, and was used in many ways by both Aborigines and early settlers.

Pittosporum phylliraeoides
(Weeping pittosporum)
fruits

Pittosporum phylliraeoides
(Weeping pittosporum)
flowers

Surianaceae

Stylobasium spathulatum

This species grows in erect bushes up to 2 m high. The flowers have a calyx cup, but no petals. There are ten stamens with large anthers which hang down below the cup. The fruit is a hard globular nut and can often be found lying underneath the shrub.

Caesalpiniaceae (cassia family)

Genus *Cassia* (cassias)

In spring, the countryside of CA-NT is covered with yellow flowering bushes. These are mostly cassias and wattles. Cassias, along with *Petalostylis* and *Bauhinia*, belong to one of the legume families. Legumes can all be identified by the finding of seeds in a pea-pod.

Cassia flowers are easily recognised. They are scented golden-yellow globular cups, with petals that are cupped and stalked. The sepals are cupped and usually yellow. The ten stamens vary in shape.

Cassia leaves are divided, each one being formed by a number of leaflets. The leaves have glands which secrete honey and attract ants. These glands can be seen as small black dots on the stems between the leaflets.

Most cassias are perennial, re-shooting from the roots and lasting about ten years. Local cassias are frost-resistant, though coastal cassias may be sensitive.

Senna is an active ingredient in both the leaves and seeds of most cassias. They therefore have a strong purgative effect and are not much eaten by either animal or man. *Cassia pleurocarpa* is the most purgative of the local cassias. The senna which is used medicinally is obtained from a cassia found in Europe

Stylobasium spathulatum – flowers

and the Mediterranean region. Because cassia species are very similar, botanists separate them mainly by their leaves. As the leaves are very variable, identification can be difficult and is made more so by hybridisation (cross-breeding).

There are about 16 species of *Cassia* found in CA-NT. Only some of them are described.

Top: Typical cassia *(C. artemisioides)* has a compound or divided leaf, with dotted line showing outline of such a leaf if simple (or entire).
Below: cupped petal with stalk or 'claw'.

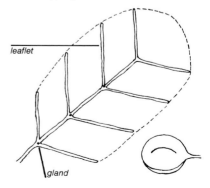

leaflet

gland

Cassia artemisioides (Silver cassia)

Cassia artemisioides (Silver cassia)

Silver cassia is a silvery shrub 1-2 m high. The leaves have 3-10 pairs of narrow leaflets which look silvery because of a dense covering of flattened white hairs. The leaflets are 1-4 cm long, terete and furrowed. The glands are between the lowest 3 pairs of leaflets. The sweetly scented flowers are in a cluster, and they have rounded petals 7-10 x 5-7 mm in size. The flat, oblong pod is 4-8 cm x 6-10 mm.

The name *artemisioides* means *like Artemis*. The plant is named after the Greek goddess Artemis, whose statue was cast in silver.

Leaf of *Cassia nemophila* (one pair of leaflets)

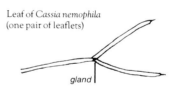

gland

Leaf of *C. nemophila* var. *platypoda* with flattened stem and leaflets.

C. nemophila (Desert cassia or Punty bush)

Desert cassia has a number of recognised varieties. In the commonest, the stems and leaflets are all terete and stem-like in shape, usually with only one pair of leaflets, which are terminal. This fork at the end of the leaf-stem is typical of the plant. There is a gland between one or more pairs of leaflets. The leaflets are hairless or sparsely haired. The pod is 2-8 cm long, 7-9 mm wide and flat. Desert cassias show much hybridisation and many forms. Some of these have become established varieties.

Desert cassia shoots very quickly after rain; both from seed and the perennial roots. It grows rapidly. As a small shrublet it can be recognised by the lush soft foliage which appears to be only stems.

It was originally intended that
C. nemophila should read *C. eremophila*, which means *desert-lover*.

Cassia nemophila (Desert cassia or Punty bush)

C. nemophila var. *platypoda*

In this variety the leaf-stem and leaflets are flattened and look like leaves. Often the two end leaflets drop off, leaving only the flattened stems or phyllodes. Usually a few of these small leaflets can be found somewhere on the bush. The name *platypoda* means *flat-foot* and refers to the flattened stem.

C. helmsii (Blunt-leaf cassia or Helm's cassia)

Helm's cassia grows 1-2 m high. The leaves are pale-grey, due to a dense covering of short and woolly hairs. There are 3-4 pairs of leaflets, which have a blunt or notched end. The glands are between the leaflets. The yellow flowers are in clusters. They are scented and cup-like, with oval petals. The pod is flat and oblong, up to 6.5 x 2 cm.

Cassia nemophila var. *platypoda*

Cassia helmsii (Blunt-leaf cassia or Helm's cassia)

C. desolata (Grey cassia)

Grey cassia is a grey-green shrub which grows 1-2 m high. There are 3-4 pairs of narrow leaflets which have a grey-green velvety covering of dense woolly hairs, and glands between the leaflets.

The scented yellow flowers are in clusters. The sepals are hairy. The flat brown pod is 5-7 x 1 cm in size. The word *desolata* means *lone,* and refers to the tendency of this species to be scattered.

Cassia desolata (Grey cassia)

C. sturtii (Dense cassia or Sturt's cassia)

This is very like Grey cassia, but may have more pairs of smaller leaflets, with a shorter leaf. The leaves are 2-4 cm long with 3-6 pairs of narrow leaflets (1-2 cm x 4 mm). The glands are between the lower leaflets. The pod is flat and hairless, 2-8 x 1 cm.

C. oligophylla (Oval-leaf cassia)

Oval-leaf cassia is a spreading bush 1-2 m high. The leaves have 1-3 pairs of leaflets which vary in shape from elliptic to almost round, with glands between the leaflets. The leaves are blue-green, either with silky flattened hairs or hairless with a waxy covering. The pods are flat and oblong, 7 x 2 cm, and may be curved.

C. pleurocarpa (Firebush, Chocolate cassia, Native senna)

Firebush or Chocolate cassia is a tough, straggly hairless shrub which suckers freely. It is often seen by the roadside and in other disturbed areas. The large leaves are 7-15 cm long and have 5-9 pairs of leaflets which are 2-5 x 1 cm, and tend to become leathery. The leaf has no glands. The chocolate-scented flowers are in erect clusters. The pod is wide and flat with transverse ridges between the seeds. It is large (4-5.5 x 1-1.6 cm). The name *pleurocarpa* means *ribbed pod*. The plant is sometimes called Native senna because of the strong purgative effect it has if eaten.

Cassia oligophylla (Oval-leaf cassia)

Cassia pleurocarpa (Firebush, Chocolate cassia, Native senna)

Cassia venusta (Graceful cassia)

C. *venusta* (Graceful cassia)

Graceful cassia grows 1-2 m high and has a covering of soft hairs. The leathery leaves are large, 10-25 cm long, with 6-15 pairs of hooked leaflets rounded at both ends. The flowers are on long strong erect stems. The notched petals are almost round, 1 cm long, and have boat-shaped sepals. The pod is flat , 5 x 1.5 cm, with transverse ridges. The word *venusta* means *graceful*.

C. *notabilis* (Cockroach bush)

C. *notabilis* is very like C. *venusta*, but is a smaller shrub. Differences are that the bush is smaller and more spreading, flowers are smaller, leaflet is barbed, and the seeds are different.

Cassia notabilis (Cockroach bush)

Genus *Petalostylis* (Butterfly bushes)

Petalostylis is closely related to the cassias. It occurs only in Australia and is widespread in the dry inland.

Petalostylis cassioides (Butterfly bush)

This is a spreading shrub which grows to 1.5 m. It has a hairy covering which may be scant or dense. The leaves have many small leaflets (23-55), which are mostly notched and sometimes hooked. The flowers are scattered in clusters of 1-3. The 5 yellow petals are slightly unequal, usually with red 'eyebrow' markings on the upper petal. In the centre there are 3 stamens, and the style projects like a boat-shaped petal. The name *petalostylis* means *petal-like style*. The brown pod is about 2.5 cm x 8 mm.

Petalostylis cassioides (Butterfly bush)

Mimosaceae (acacia family)

Genus *Acacia* (wattles)

Acacias are native to Africa, Australia, Papua New Guinea and South America, in the tropical areas and southwards. They are widespread in Australia and provide the main tree covering in very arid regions. A large percentage of the world's acacias are native to Australia, about 800 of 1200 species. The flowers are our national floral emblem. The Australian name for *Acacia* is wattle. The name wattle is derived from an Anglo-Saxon word *watel* meaning *interlacing twigs,* and arose from the wattle-and-daub buildings of the early settlers. The word *akakia* is an Egyptian word for *thorn-bush,* and refers to an Egyptian species which has very long thorns. Many Australian species are grown commercially in other countries for wood, tannin, gum arabic, shellac and lacquer, as well as for sand stabilisation. In some places they have grown so well they have become weeds.

Of the 800 or so Australian species, over 100 occur naturally in the dry inland. They are widely used as cattle fodder and for their wood. Aborigines obtained food from wattles both directly and indirectly. The seeds of some wattles are edible as flour, and others have nourishing gum. Grubs are found in roots and galls, and honey is obtained from mulga by honey-pot mulga ants. The woods of Mulga, Gidgee and Southern ironwood are hard and decorative. Mulga foliage is a good stock food; however *Acacia georginae* [Georgina gidgee] is very poisonous in certain localities.

Wattle flowers

Wattle flowers are individually very tiny, and are packed together in flower heads which are shaped like balls or spikes. The individual flowers can be seen as small knobs in the bud. The flower heads may contain up to 50-100 flowers. Each flower has small sepals and petals, and 5 long stamens. The characteristics of the flower are constant for each species.

Wattle leaves

Most Australian acacias have their leaves replaced by phyllodes, with true leaves only in the seedling stage. Phyllodes are flattened leaf-stems which function as leaves. The phyllodes (stems) have less pores than leaves and the pores are sunken and tougher and therefore lose less moisture. The phyllodes often have parallel veins, though some have a leaf-like central vein. There is only one wattle with true leaves found in CA-NT. For the sake of simplicity, wattle phyllodes will be called leaves in this publication. Wattle 'leaves' have one or more glands which can be seen on the edge of the leaf. The gland-opening is pinhole size, and often near the base or the tip of a leaf. These glands provide nectar for ants and some birds.

Pods and Seeds

Each species has pods of relatively constant size, shape and texture. Pods often remain on the bush or under it and can be collected to help in identification. Seeds are on fleshy stalks which are often brightly coloured. This colour attracts insects and birds and so aids in seed distribution. Seeds also fall or sometimes shoot out from the pods. The seeds have a strong protective covering and can lie dormant many years before germination. To grow the seeds the gardener must soak them in hot water to soften the coat.

Roots

Wattles may be shallow-rooted, but the roots can sometimes spread very deep: some have been found 12 m underground. Most species depend on seedlings for reproduction, but suckering occurs in some species. Like other legumes, acacias develop root nodules which can extract free nitrogen from the soil. This helps them to survive in nitrogen deficient soils typical of arid Australia. This process depends on the presence of a special strain of *Rhizobium* bacteria in the nodules.

Insects

Insects eat away at acacias constantly, but there seems to be a natural balance maintained. Ants are very active on wattles, cleaning fungus away and getting rid of competing insects, but they act as protectors for those insects which excrete honeydew.

Grouping wattles

Wattles can be grouped according to the shape of the flower heads and the character of the leaves. Those with spiked flower heads only have leaves with parallel veins. Those with globular flower heads may have the following:
> no leaves
> leaves in bundles or whorls
> leaves terete or quadrangular
> leaves flat with a central vein
> leaves with parallel veins.

Whatever grouping is used there will be some overlapping, due mainly to variations in leaf. Confusion is also caused because hybridisation occurs in the natural state – closely related wattles often produce hybrids. About 75 different wattles occur in CA-NT. Only some of these will be described here.

Globular flower heads – no leaves

Acacia wiseana

This leafless wattle is found only in the Tanami Desert. It is a bright-green intricately branched shrub up to 3 m high, with strongly scented branchlets. There may be a few leaves, but these drop early. The flower heads are globular, and the twisted papery pod is 18 x 1 cm.

Globular flower heads – leaves in bundles or whorls

A. tetragonophylla (Dead finish)

Dead finish is a straggly bush about 2 m high, which grows throughout the deserts of Australia. The four-sided needle-like leaves are short with needle-sharp points, and are in clusters of 3-5. The name *tetragonophylla* means *four-sided leaf.* The golden globular flower heads are carried on individual stalks and each head has about 50 tiny flowers. The pods are narrow and twisted with constrictions between the seeds. They are up to 13 cm long.
The Aborigines used to grind the seed for cakes, and made a cough medicine by soaking the roots and bark.

Acacia tetragonophylla (Dead finish)

A. spondylophylla (Curry wattle, Spineleaf wattle)

Curry wattle grows only 50 cm-1 m high, but spreads sideways for some distance. It grows on hillslopes in rocky areas, and is often hidden amongst the spinifex. The bush produces a strong scent of curry. The smell comes from a sticky exudate which covers stems, leaves and pods. The leaves are about 1 cm long, in whorls of 8-14, and have hooked pointed ends. The globular flower heads are carried on individual stalks which are longer than the leaves. The bright-green pods are twisted, very sticky, and raised over each seed.

Acacia spondyophylla (Curry wattle, Spineleaf wattle)

Globular flower heads
– leaves terete or quadrangular

A. peuce (Waddy wood)

This drooping needle-leaf wattle occurs in only a few places. There is one group of trees in the south-west Simpson Desert at Andado, and another near Birdsville. The word *peuce* is Greek for *pine*, and the trees can easily be mistaken for pines or casuarina. The distinguishing feature is the seed pod.

The long narrow drooping leaves are square in cross-section and end in a point. They are up to 40 cm long and only 1 mm wide. The young tree is a different shape to the adult, and has many twiggy branches which point outwards. The flower heads are globular. The pods are up to 20 x 3 cm, whitish, papery and twisted when dry.

Globular flower heads
– leaves flat with a central vein

A. maitlandii (Maitland's wattle)

This shrubby wattle is scented and very sticky, and has spiky leaves. The scent comes from a resin which exudes from the smooth hairless stems and leaves. The globular flower heads are dense (50-60 flowers per head) and individually stalked. The pods are straight and narrow, 2-3 cm long, and constricted around the seeds. Maitland's wattle grows on sand plains and dunes. The seed was eaten by the Aborigines after grinding it to make flour.

Acacia maitlandii (Maitland's wattle)

Acacia maitlandii (Maitland's wattle) (enlarged) – note resin on stems

A. strongylophylla (Round-leaf wattle)

This bush grows in rocky gorges and
waterways. It can be seen on the rocky
hillsides at the Olgas, also at Standley
Chasm, and is common at Arltunga.
The name *strongylophylla* means
rounded leaves. The stems and leaves
are hairless and there are spines at the
base of the leaf. The blue-green leaves
are round with a central vein and pointed
tip. The large globular flower heads each
have up to 50 flowers. The papery pods
are flat and straight, up to 8 x 1 cm.

A. inaequilatera (Fire wattle)

These small gnarled trees have corky
bark and bluish-white stems. The leaves
are oval, up to 7 x 3.5 cm, with a pointed
spiny tip and one prominent vein to one
side of the midline. The golden globular
flower heads are on red stems. The pods
are curved. There is a stand of these
wattles at the western side of the Olgas.

Acacia strongylophylla (Round-leaf wattle)

A. victoriae (Acacia bush, Victoria wattle)

Victoria wattle was named after the Victoria River in Queensland where it was first found. It is commonly called Acacia bush. In the NT it is widespread and can be found as far north as the Victoria River in the NT. It is a bush or small untidy tree which grows in thickets. The branches are often green and the foliage is more blue-green than many inland wattles. Many of the trees have stem prickles, but these may be absent. The leaves have a central vein, and are flat, narrow and pointed. After rain in winter or spring the tree grows long graceful flowering branches. The globular flower heads are delicate cream. The pods are papery, flat and oblong, about 6 cm long.

Acacia bush is widespread and is an important fodder tree. It regenerates well, although it dies in severe droughts. It can be seen on the sand plains whichever way one travels from Alice Springs. For the Aborigines it provided edible seed and gum – and was also used as a glue.

Acacia victoriae (Acacia bush, Victoria wattle)

Acacia victoriae (Acacia bush, Victoria wattle) in flower

A. murrayana (Colony wattle,
Murray wattle)

This small tree grows extensively in
colonies, and is often found with Acacia
bush. The colonies develop mainly from
root suckering. Seeding is also prolific,
but germination occurs mainly after fire.
The tree trunks are mostly greyish-white
due to a white waxy covering. The leaves
are long and narrow (5-18 cm x 2-10 mm),
with a central vein. They point outwards.
The globular flower heads are deep golden
and contain 25-50 flowers. The heads
are in clusters. The papery pods are flat,
raised over the seeds and up to 8 x 1 cm
in size. Colony wattle is not palatable
to cattle.

A. ligulata (Umbrella bush)

Umbrella bush is a small dome-
shaped ground hugging wattle which
usually has the appearance of being
much chewed by insects. There are
many different predators, but a natural
balance is maintained, with ants playing
an important role. The young leaves are
long, narrow and succulent; the older
leaves shorter, wider and leathery.
They vary from 3-10 cm x 2-20 mm, have
a central vein and a blunt hooked end.
The globular golden flower heads have
18-28 flowers. The pods are long and
twisted, and constricted between the
seeds. There is a bright-red seed stalk
which attracts birds. The word *ligule*
means *tongue* and refers to this seed stalk.
The Aborigines obtained food from the
seed and the gum. They also used the
ashes to mix with pituri, which they
used as a narcotic.

This small wattle is widespread in
CA-NT. It can be seen at Rainbow
Valley, along the Glen Helen road
and beyond, and in the dune country.
It is also seen east and south of Alice
Springs. It is useful in helping stabilise
sand areas as it regenerates well and
grows quickly. It is unpalatable to cattle.

Acacia murrayana (Colony wattle, Murray wattle)

Acacia ligulata (Umbrella bush) seed pods

Acacia ligulata (Umbrella bush) flowers

Acacia ligulata (Umbrella bush)

A. salicina (Cooba, Native willow)

This graceful weeping wattle is closely related to *A. ligulata*. The leaves are dark-green, about 7 x 1 cm, with a central vein and pointed ends. The mature tree looks rather like *A. estrophiolata* (Ironwood). The globular flower heads hang in loose clusters. They are delicate cream, with only 15-25 flowers per head. The pods differ from umbrella bush and from ironwood. They are straight, rounded and light-brown, 6-12 x 1 cm, with no constrictions. The seeds have thick scarlet stalks. This wattle is widespread in CA-NT and is often found along water courses.

Acacia salicina (Cooba, Native willow)

A. pruinocarpa (Black gidgee, Black wattle)

Black wattle is usually found in deep sand country, especially west from Alice Springs. The stems have a whitish sheen and the foliage is a dull dark-green. The leaves are large, 17 x 2 cm, often curved, and have a strong central vein. The golden globular flower heads have 50-100 flowers per head. The pods are whitish. They are about 12 cm long, straight and flat. The name *pruinocarpa* means *pods with white sheen.*

Acacia pruinocarpa (Black gidgee, Black wattle)

Globular flower heads
– leaves with parallel veins

A. *dictyophleba* (Waxy wattle, Sandhill wattle, Feather-veined wattle)

This small shrubby wattle can be recognised by the white waxy patches on its leaves. The word *dictyophleba* means *feather-veined*. The feather-like veining can be seen by holding a leaf against the light. The globular flower heads each contain 60-80 flowers. The pods are straight, flat and narrow, about 9 cm long. The seed was ground and eaten by the Aborigines. This wattle is widespread in CA-NT. The name Sandhill wattle is also used for several other species.

Acacia dictyophleba (Waxy wattle, Sandhill wattle, Feather-veined wattle)

A. *estrophiolata* (Ironwood)

This graceful weeping tree is one of the larger of our inland trees. It grows prolifically in and around Alice Springs and southwards, but is not found north of Tennant Creek. The long drooping branches hang down like a willow. The flat leaves are narrow, 4-11 cm x 2-4 mm, with parallel veins. The globular flower heads are pale yellow. The narrow pods are constricted between the seeds. The young tree first has an erect stage before becoming a drooping mature tree. These young trees have leaves which are shorter and often clustered. Ironwood is an important cattle fodder. The wood is very hard and is used for fencing. The sugary gum was an Aboriginal food staple. The name Ironwood is used for a number of different kinds of Australian tree, so the common name needs to be qualified by the botanical.

Acacia estrophiolata (Ironwood)

Acacia estrophiolata (Ironwood) flowers

A. *coriacea* (Dogwood)

Dogwood is a shrubby small tree found mainly in deep sand in the dune country. From a distance it can look like a *Grevillea striata* (Beefwood) because of similar long strap-like leaves which point outwards. The name *coriacea* means *leathery.* The long narrow leaves are leathery and may be flat or almost terete. The leaves appear silvery due to a covering of fine flattened hairs, and new growth can be golden. The yellow globular flower heads are small, 5 mm in diameter, and have only 20-25 flowers per head. The pods are long, narrow and twisted, and look silvery-white. They are about 20 x 1 cm. The seeds were much sought after by the Aborigines, who ate them as a vegetable, and also ground them for flour. They are still enjoyed when available. In CA-NT the leaves and pods are not very palatable to stock although sheep graze them in Queensland.

Acacia coriacea (Dogwood)

A. cambagei (Gidgee, Stinking wattle)

Like mulga this wattle usually grows in stands and is found over a large area of the dry inland. The tree grows 5-10 m high, has brown furrowed bark and erect spreading branches. The curved leaves are grey-green, and often look silvery, due to a white iridescence and to fine hairs. The leaves have parallel veins and pointed ends, and are about 10 x 1 cm. When the leaves are crushed they give off a strong unpleasant smell which wafts about, especially in humid weather. The flower heads are globular with 12-25 flowers.

The pods are papery, straight-edged and flat, about 7 cm long (Georgina gidgee has spiralling pods). The seeds are longitudinal in the pod (Georgina gidgee has seeds transverse or oblique). *A. cambagei* (Gidgee, Stinking wattle) is not poisonous like Georgina gidgee, but it is not very palatable to stock although it does provide forage at times. The wood is a good fuel. The wood is hard and heavy, good for building and fences, and valued by the Aborigines for weapons.

Acacia cambagei (Gidgee, Stinking wattle)

A. georginae (Georgina gidgee)

Georgina gidgee is very similar to
A. cambagei. It is spread through the
Georgina River basin in Queensland
and the adjacent part of the NT, north,
south and east of Alice Springs. It is a
smaller bushy tree, up to 5 m high, sometimes with multiple stems, and has a
dense silvery canopy. It is noted for being
very poisonous to stock, but it has now
been found that poisoning occurs only in
certain places and in other places it can
be used for fodder. The leaves are similar
to those of *A. cambagei*, but are straighter
and more leathery. The pods are spiralled
not straight, and the seeds are transverse
or oblique in the pod. This species also
gives out a stinking smell at times.

Acacia georginae (Georgina gidgee)

Spiked flower heads – leaves with parallel veins

A. aneura (Mulga)

Mulga grows as a grey-green bush or small tree, and covers wide areas of arid inland Australia. It is one of the best survivors in poor conditions, and provides nutritious topfeed for cattle, making cattle-runs possible in marginal country. The wood is both ornamental and hard and is still in use for artefacts and weapons for the tourist market and fences etc. in cattle yards. The small untidy tree often looks grey with silvery tips, and freshens to grey-green after rain. In desert areas it has a brownish colour. The trees grow in stands, with seedlings growing in the shade of mature trees. Young trees are shaped like small pine trees. As the tree matures the canopy branches spread out and the twiggy side stems fall off. The leaves point up and out and so catch every drop of moisture. They are very variable in shape, from small and needle-like to larger and wider, 1-17 cm x 1-8 mm. There are many variants, but all are considered to be the same species. The flower spikes are cylindrical. The papery pods are short and flat, 1.5-5 cm x 4-15 mm. Mulga trees often have mistletoes, which do not seem to affect them when conditions are good. The Aborigines used to grind mulga seed to make cakes. They also relish the mulga apple, which is an insect gall about the size of an cherry. Aborigines still eat honey-pot ants, which store honey in their bodies. This honey is obtained mainly from mulgas.

Acacia aneura (Mulga)

Acacia aneura (Mulga) bloom

A. ammobia

This small wattle of the sandhills is quite like Mulga. The leaves have parallel veins and are hairless with a waxy covering. The flowers are in spikes. The pods are long and narrow, 11 cm x 2 mm, and slightly constricted between the seeds.

A. ayersiana (Ayers Rock mulga)

This wattle grows as a large bush up to 8 m high. It is closely allied to A. aneura (Mulga), and looks rather like a large witchetty bush. The grey-green leaves have parallel veins and are slightly curved. The flowers are in spikes and the pods are short and flat, up to 3 x 1.8 cm.

A. brachystachya group

including A. ramulosa (Horse mulga) and A. brachystachya (Umbrella wattle)

These are bushy shrubs or spreading trees found growing with common mulga, and can not always be distinguished. The leaves have parallel veins and a fine hairy covering. The flowers are in spikes. The flat or cylindrical pods hang down, and look pale because of a hairy covering.

A. olgana (Mt Olga wattle)

This spreading bushy tree is found in the gorges and outcrops of Mt Olga. It can be seen in the Olga Gorge. The bright-green leaves are long and narrow and curved at the ends. They are hairless, although new shoots have fine golden hairs. The leaves have parallel veins. The flowers are in golden spikes, and the paper pods are straight and narrow, 10 cm x 7 mm.

Acacia olgana (Mt Olga wattle)

83

A. *ancistrocarpa* (Fitzroy wattle)

This wattle is an erect bush 2-3 m high. The bright green leaves point upwards, and have parallel veins with a strong central vein. The flowers are in yellow cylindrical spikes. The brown pods are straight and narrow, up to 9 x 1 cm. Fitzroy wattle is found on sand plains in central and northern CA-NT.

A. *kempeana* (Witchetty bush)

Witchetty bush is a spreading shrub or tree up to 4 m tall. The grey-green leaves are curved, about 7 x 1 cm, with parallel veins and rounded ends. The flower heads are golden spikes. The papery pods are flat, about 7 x 1 cm.

The Aborigines obtain witchetty grubs from the roots. The grub is eaten raw or slightly roasted, and has a nutty flavour. It is highly nourishing and was used as a baby food. The Witchetty bush also has edible gum and seed. It is only grazed lightly in good seasons, but is valuable topfeed for cattle in droughts.

Acacia ancistrocarpa (Fitzroy wattle)

Acacia kempeana (Witchetty bush)

Acacia kempeana (Witchetty bush)

A. macdonnelliensis (MacDonnell mulga)

This erect bushy wattle is found in the rocky range of CA-NT. The leaves are narrow, 6-15 cm x 1-3 mm, sometimes terete, with fine parallel veins and hooked ends. The flowers are in large cylindrical spikes. The pods are narrow, 7.5 cm x 2-4 mm.

A. holosericea (Candelabra wattle)

The name *holosericea* means *wholly clothed in silk.* This wattle is covered with silky hairs. The leaf is large, wide and pointed, 15 x 5 cm, with parallel veins. The flower spikes are narrow, and 3-6 cm long. The papery pods are curved or coiled, and constricted between the seeds. The ground-up seeds were a food staple of the Aborigines. The leaves and bark were soaked to make a bush medicine for coughs and colds.

Acacia macdonnelliensis (MacDonnell mulga)

Wattle with true leaves

A. farnesiana (Mimosa bush, Prickly moses)

This species grows in all parts of the world where acacias grow. It was probably introduced to Australia thousands of years ago. It has been cultivated in France since the seventeenth century, and is called after the gardens where it was first planted in Europe. It is grown for the perfume industry. Its bark, gum and juice have been used medicinally in the countries where it grows naturally. In CA-NT it is often seen growing as small spiky bushes lining the banks of dry creeks. It also grows into taller prickly bushes on the flood-out areas of rivers. It can be distinguished by its ferny leaves, vicious prickles, and

Acacia holosericea (Candelabra wattle)

black pods. This is the only inland wattle with true leaves. The leaves are much-divided, giving a fern-like appearance. The sweet-scented flower heads are large (at least 1 cm in diameter), globular, and are carried on individual stalks. The green fleshy pods become black when ripe, and often remain on the bush. Cattle enjoy the foliage, and sheep the pods. The Aborigines ate the ground-up seed, and also the gum.

Acacia farnesiana (Mimosa bush, Prickly moses)

Fabaceae (keeled pea-flower family)

There are three families belonging to the legume group. These are Fabaceae (keeled peas), Mimosaceae (acacias), and Caesalpinaceae (cassias). All of these have their seeds in a pod which is called a legume. In a legume the seeds are in a row, hanging from the central seam or hinge of the pod which opens along the opposite seam. Other seed-cases are sometimes called pods, but only the legume families have pods of the pea-pod type.

Fabaceae, like all legumes, have the seeds in a hinged pod. Peas and beans are two of the best known keeled pea species. The flower has 5 petals: the back petal stands erect and is called the *standard*, the two lowest petals join to form the *keel*, and the two side petals are called *wings*.

Fabaceae include over 10,000 species, which are found throughout the world. The family includes many species which are important commercially. They are used as foods, for animal fodder, in medicines, and also form valuable crops for soil enrichment. Alfalfa, clover and lucerne are keeled peas, as are various vegetables, and garden ornamentals such as wisteria, lupins and sweetpeas. The family is widespread in the dry inland of Australia

Fabaceae – Keeled peas

Keeled pea flower

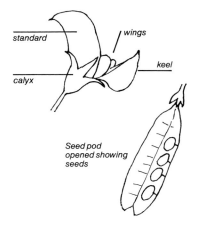

standard

wings

keel

calyx

Seed pod opened showing seeds

where peas thrive in many different situations. Fabaceae can develop root-nodules which use *Rhizobium* bacteria to fix nitrogen from the soil and enables plants to succeed in poor soils. Like other families, peas are divided into genera according to specific character-istics, such as variations in shape and detail. Identification by microscopic detail is outside the scope of this book, and only the more obvious character-istics will be described.

Genus *Gastrolobium*

Gastrolobium species grow as shrubs with flat leathery opposite leaves. The flowers are red and yellow. The name *gastrolobium* means *belly-shaped pod*. The seed-pods are round or egg-shaped and 1-2 cm long.

Gastrolobium grandiflorum (Wallflower poison bush)

Wallflower poison bush grows to 1.5 m in height. The oblong leaves have notched rounded ends and are 3-6 cm long. The red and yellow flowers are about 2 cm long. The calyx is hairy and the pod stalked. The name *grandiflorum* means *stately or large flower.* The plant is poisonous to horses, killing those belonging to the explorer John McDouall Stuart, during his overland crossing.

G. brevipes

This plant is very similar to G. *grandi-florum.* It grows up to 1 m high, and is found in the central ranges and south-wards. The oblong leathery leaves have notched ends and are about 1 cm wide. The red and yellow flowers are 1-1.5 cm long. The name *brevipes* means *short foot* and refers to the pod having no stalk.

Gastrolobium brevipes

Genus *Isotropis*

The *Isotropis* group are small shrubby plants. Some species are poisonous to stock. The word *isotropis* comes from Greek and means *equal keel*. This refers to the flower, in which the wings are about the same size as the keel. The flowers are red to orange and have a large rounded standard petal with a central notch. The leaves are simple (not divided), and the leaf-stalk may be jointed. The pod is oblong. There are 3 *Isotropis* species found in CA-NT.

Isotropis centralis

This *Isotropis* is found only in a few small creeks in the central and south-west ranges. It is found in the Olgas. The small shrubby bush grows only to 20 cm high. It is rusty pale-green due to a covering of rusty-coloured hairs. The pale-green hairy leaves are wide with undulating edges, and about 1 cm long. The leaf stalk is jointed. The flowers are about 1 cm long, bright-red and striated. The small oblong pods are about 1.5 cm long, and hairy.

This plant is not recorded as a danger to stock as it grows in inaccessible places.

I. atropurpurea (Poison sage)

Poison sage grows to the north of Alice Springs and has caused stock poisoning in the past when it occurred prolifically around bores used by travelling stock. It is similar to *I. centralis*, but is a larger bush. The name *atropurpurea* means *deep purple*, and the flowers are red to purple. The leaves are round to oblong, 1-3 x 1 cm. Leaves, stems, calyx and pod are all hairy. The oblong pod is up to 2.5 cm long.

Isotropis centralis

Right: Flower of
Isotropis centralis
showing standard petal,
striated and notched.
Below: Leaf (left) and pod.

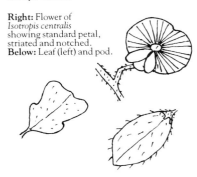

Isotropis centralis

Genus *Leptosema*
(previously called *Brachysema*)

Leptosemas are small shrubs, some of which have their leaves reduced to scales. The flowers spread along stems at the base of the plant, and the standard is much shorter than the wings or keel. The name *leptosema* means *slender standard*. There are 2 *Leptosema* species in CA-NT.

Leptosema chambersii (Chambers leptosema, Upside-down-plant)

This small shrubby bush is found amongst the spinifex, and grows to 20-40 cm high. It has no ordinary leaves, but consists of smooth much-branched stems which are sometimes spiny where the leaf remnants are. The stalked flowers are spread along stems which emerge from the base of the plant. The large bright-red flowers are over 4 cm long. They do not look like typical pea flowers because the wing and keel petals are long with the short narrow standard hidden behind them.

The velvety calyx has long pointed teeth. The pods are about 12 cm long, beaked, and have a velvety covering. When in flower this is a very striking plant. It is sometimes called 'the Upside-down-plant' because the flowers are at the bottom. The flowers produce abundant nectar and the Aborigines used it as a food.

L. anomalum

This species is found in northern CA-NT.

Leptosema chambersii (Chambers leptosema, Upside-down-plant)

Genus *Crotalaria*

The name *crotalaria* comes from a Greek-Latin word meaning *a rattle* or *castanet*, which refers to the fact that the seeds rattle in the pod. The leaves either have 3 leaflets or 1 leaflet on a jointed stem. The flowers are usually yellow. The flower has a beaked keel which is longer than the wing petals. The pods are inflated and rattle when dry.

There are 9 species of *Crotalaria* to be found in CA-NT. Some of them are poisonous to stock.

Crotalaria cunninghamii (Parrot pea, Cunningham's rattlepod)

This crotalaria has a large yellow-green flower which is shaped like a bird. The straggly shrub is about 1 m high, and is found in sand-dune country, usually on the dunes. The plant has a large root system which binds the sand, and it can shoot from the roots. The stems are thick and pithy, and the surface of the plant is covered with long soft hairs. The thick soft leaves are about 7 x 3 cm. The flowers are up to 6 cm long, and have yellow-green petals with purple striations. The keel is beaked and longer than the wing petals. The pods are inflated.

Crotalaria cunninghamii (Parrot pea, Cunningham's rattlepod)

C. eremaea (Desert rattlepod, Bluebush pea)

Desert rattlepod is a common pea of dry areas, and is often seen on the roadside. The name *eremaea* means *desert-lover*. There are 2 different leaf forms. One has 3 narrow leaflets with the basal leaflets short. The other has only 1 leaflet. There are variations between these 2 forms.

The surface varies from finely-haired to almost hairless. The flowers are 1-2 cm long. They are stalked and spaced out on long spikes. The pods are club-shaped, up to 3 cm long.

Crotalaria eremaea (Desert rattlepod) – leaf variations

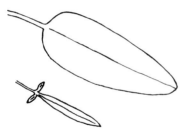

Crotalaria eremaea (Desert rattlepod, Bluebush pea)

C. dissitiflora (Grey rattlepod)

This small yellow-flowered pea bush is very similar to desert rattlepod. It also is found in disturbed areas such as by the roadside. It is a hairy perennial with extensive underground roots. The leaf usually has 3 leaflets with the basal leaflets at least half as long as the terminal. The yellow flowers are stalked, and spaced out along the stems to form spikes. The name *dissitiflora* means *spaced flowers*. The club-shaped pod is up to 3 cm long. In eastern States this pea is considered poisonous to sheep.

Crotalaria dissitiflora (Grey rattlepod)

C. novae-hollandiae (New-Holland rattlepod)

New-Holland rattlepod is an untidy many-stemmed bush about 1 m high. The thick velvety leaves turn up at their sides and are 2-8 cm long. They are often wrinkled which makes them look pleated. The yellow flower spikes are on sturdy erect stems, and are up to 25 cm long. The pod is 3-4 cm long.

C. smithiana – also called *C. mitchellii* (Yellow rattlepod)

Yellow rattlepod grows to 30 cm. It is grey to blue-green due to a covering of long soft hairs. The velvety leaves are about 5 x 3 cm. The yellow flower spikes are erect, and up to 14 cm long. The inflated pod is oblong.

Crotalaria novae-hollandiae (New-Holland rattlepod)

Genus *Daviesia* (Broom bushes)

Daviesia are much-branched shrubs with leaves which may be simple or stem-like, or reduced to scales. The pods have a flattened triangular shape. There are two *Daviesia* species found in CA-NT.

D. arthropoda

This species is similar to *D. eremaea*, but it has flat narrow leaves which are 5-35 mm long, and widest at the end.

Daviesia eremaea (Desert broom bush)

This is a many-stemmed bush 1-2 m tall. The scented leaves are rigid, terete, stem-like and pointed. They are 3-15 mm long. Leaves may be absent. The pea flowers are yellow and brown. The flower stalks are 5-7 mm long and the flattened triangular pods are 7-9 mm long. Broom bush is found on sandplains with spinifex and desert oak.

Daviesia eremaea (Desert broom bush)

Genus *Tephrosia*

The name *tephrosia* comes from the Greek *tephros* meaning *ash-coloured*. This refers to the grey hairy covering that most species of *Tephrosia* have. The leaves are usually compound with the leaflets in pairs and a larger end leaflet. The flowers are orange, pink or purple and are in small clusters. The pod is usually straight and narrow-oblong.

There are 6 species of *Tephrosia* found in CA-NT.

Tephrosia brachydon

This small *Tephrosia* has a leaf with 5-11 narrow leaflets which hang downwards. The rose-pink flowers are 5-8 mm long on short stalks in clusters of 3. The pod is flattened, narrow, and straight with a curve at the end.

Genus *Indigofera*

Indigofera is the genus from which the blue dye indigo is obtained. This dye has a long history of use and it continues to be used by the Chinese for their present-day clothing. A similar synthetic dye is used for the colour of denim jeans. Australian indigos do not produce a useful dye.

Indigoferas are usually small shrubs with grey or white hairy covering. The compound leaves have up to 21 leaflets. The flowers are purple or red and are in spikes which stand up from the bush. The hairy pod is usually narrow-oblong.

There are 12 species of *Indigofera* found in CA-NT.

Indigofera basedowii (Showy indigo, Basedow's indigo)

This small shrub is covered with short grey hairs. The leaves have 7-21 velvety leaflets which are elliptic to oblong, and hooked. The purple flowers are in strong erect spikes 4-11 cm long. The buds and

Tephrosia brachydon

Indigofera basedowii (Showy indigo, Basedow's indigo)

94

calyx look black due to a covering of long black hairs. The cylindrical pod is straight and narrow. Showy indigo is found in gorges and at the bottom of rocky hills, and can be seen at the Olgas.

I. georgei (Georges indigo)

This velvety low bushy shrub is densely covered with short hairs. It is found in rocky water-courses and can be seen at Standley Chasm. The leaf has 5-7 velvety leaflets which are blue-grey because of their hairy covering. The flower spikes can be lilac or red and the erect spikes are 5-25 cm long. The calyx is hairy with black and grey hairs. The pod is long and narrow.

Indigofera georgei (Georges indigo)

I. leucotricha (White indigo)

This whitish shrub is often dry and brittle. It is seen on rocky hillsides, often in company with Freeling's eremophila, and can be seen in the Finke River Gorge, Palm Valley, and Ndhala Gorge. It copes with dry spells by dropping leaves and drying out, and re-shoots after rain. The untidy low bush is covered with white hairs which give it its white appearance. The name *leucotricha* means *white hairs*. The leaves have 9-13 small leaflets. The small red pea flowers are in short spikes 3-6 cm long. The narrow pod is hairy.

Indigofera leucotricha (White indigo)

Indigofera linifolia (Native indigo)

I. linifolia (Native indigo)

This low spreading plant has narrow leaves 2-5 cm x 2-4 mm. The red flowers are only 2-4 mm long and are in small clusters. The tiny globular pods are about 2 mm long.

I. linnaei – also called *I. enneaphylla*, *I. dominii* (Birdsville indigo)

Birdsville indigo is a low spreading plant which is becoming widespread in CA-NT where it is a problem because it causes poisoning in horses. It is a perennial with extensive roots. It shoots quickly after rain and the tender shoots are tempting to hungry stock. Sheep and goats are not poisoned by it, however, and if they are available can be used to clear a paddock for horses.

The silky compound leaves have 7-9 leaflets. The small red pea flowers are in rosette-like clusters at the angle between the leaf and the stem. The silky pods are only 2 mm long.

Indigofera linnaei – also called *I. enneaphylla*, *I. dominii* (Birdsville indigo)

Genus *Clianthus*

The only Australian species of *Clianthus* is Sturt desert pea. The name *clianthus* comes from the Greek *kleos* meaning *glory* and *anthos* meaning *flower*. The most striking feature of *Clianthus* is the large flower which is always over 4 cm long. The pods are swollen.

Clianthus formosus (Sturt desert pea)

The name *formosus* means *finely formed* or *elegant*. Sturt desert pea is an annual or biennial which grows prostrate, spreading across the ground and sending the flower clusters erect. The plant is grey-green due to a hairy covering. The stems are thick and pithy. The large leaves are divided into oval leaflets each 1-3 cm long. The large red flowers are up to 9 cm from tip to tip. The standard petal is pointed and has a shiny black or red dome at the base. The keel is the same length and points downwards. The wing petals are smaller. The flowers are held erect in groups of 3 or more, on strong stems which come off at right-angles to the leaf-stem.

Sturt desert pea is much sought after as a garden plant. The seeds need to be soaked in hot water overnight and nicked, to assist in germination. Once established the plant thrives best if not watered too much.

Sturt desert pea is found in the desert areas of Australia, mainly in places where grazing has not occurred. It is quickly eaten out by cattle. It is quite rare in the NT, but more common to the south.

Clianthus formosus – flower

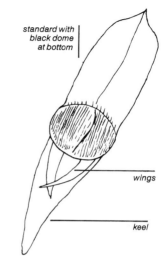

Clianthus formosus (Sturt desert pea)

Genus *Swainsona*

In CA-NT, swainsonas are often called vetches because, like the vetch (genus *Vicia)*, they are creeping purple peas. Some swainsonas are shrubs, but many are prostrate and spread across the ground sending their flower-stems upwards. There are annuals and perennials. They vary from hairy to hairless. The compound leaves usually have many small leaflets. The small pea flowers are usually purple, red or blue, with a yellow patch near the base of the standard. The keel is broad. The pod can be inflated or leathery and may have a furrow at the suture line.

There are 16 *Swainsona* species found in CA-NT.

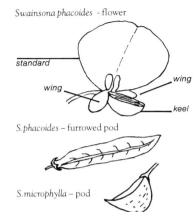

Swainsona phacoides - flower

standard

wing

wing

keel

S.phacoides – furrowed pod

S.microphylla – pod

Swainsona phacoides (Dwarf swainsona)

Swainsona phacoides (Dwarf swainsona)

This low spreading plant is covered with soft hairs which vary from flattened to spreading. The purple flowers are held erect in clusters of about 6, on the ends of stems about 20 cm long. The leaves have 5-13 leaflets. The cylindrical pod is 1-3 cm long, with a deep furrow.

S. microphylla (Small-leafed swainsona, Poison pea)

The word *microphylla* means *small leafed*. *S. microphylla* is also called Poison pea, because it is poisonous to stock though not frequently grazed. There are a number of subspecies which vary in hairiness, leaflets and flower colour. All have numerous small leaflets which are often notched. There are 11-41 leaflets which are each 2-9 mm long. The small stalked flowers are in spikes which stand erect. They are usually purple or blue, but may be yellow or white. The flower-stalk and calyx both have brown hairs. The pods are inflated, almost round, with a beaked end.

Swainsona microphylla (Small-leafed swainsona, Poison pea) – purple flowers are reddened by late afternoon light.

Swainsona microcalyx

S. microcalyx

This small swainsona is sparsely covered
by short flattened hairs. The leaves have
7-9 leaflets. The flowers are in clusters
of 6-15, and the calyx cup is small
(3-5 mm long). The pod is 2 cm x 4 mm,
with a furrowed suture line.

S. burkei (Burke swainsona)

This low hairy shrub spreads across
the ground sending its flower-stems
15-30 cm upwards. The compound
leaves have 8-20 leaflets each about
1 cm long. There are 2 subspecies
which have different shaped flowers.
Subspecies *burkei* has triangular wings
and a blunt keel. Subspecies *acuticarinata*
has rounded wings and a pointed keel.
The flowers are in clusters of about 6.
The pods are oblong and deeply
furrowed.

Swainsona burkei ssp. *acuticarinata*
(Burke swainsona)

S. flavicarinata (Yellow-keeled swainsona)

This small plant spreads across the ground and sends its flower-stems upwards, each with 10 or so multi-coloured flowers. The plant is grey-green due to a covering of long soft hairs. The leaves have 5-9 leaflets which are hairless above and hairy beneath. The flowers are usually blue, red or purple, with a yellow keel. The name *flavicarinata* means *yellow keel.* The pod is deeply furrowed.

Swainsona flavicarinata
(Yellow-keeled swainsona)

S. cyclocarpa

This small pea is found in salty areas such as clay-pans and near salt-lakes. The plant is sparsely covered with short flattened hairs and the leaflets are hairless above. The leaves have 5-11 leaflets which are wide with a rounded end. The flowers are in clusters of 8-15. The pod is crescent-shaped with uneven ridges running transversely.

Swainsona cyclocarpa

Genus *Psoralea*

The name *psoralea* comes from the Greek *psoraleos* meaning *scabby*. Psoraleas are shrubby erect bushes with long spreading branches. They vary from hairy to hairless, and are dotted with glands. The leaves have 3 leaflets which are often toothed. The small flowers may be pink, blue or white. They are on very short stalks in a long narrow spike, with a long flower-stem.

There are 15 species in Australia, 8 in CA-NT.

Psoralea patens (Native verbine)

This shrubby plant has long spreading stems, and is covered by soft hairs. The leaves have 3 stalked leaflets which are pointed and toothed. They are up to 2 cm in size and have a rough scabby surface. The small pink flowers are clustered closely in a long spike on the end of a stem which may be up to 27 cm long. The small flowers have almost no stalks. The calyx is covered with long silky black or white hairs. It is 3-6 mm long with flowers longer by only 1-2 mm. The small black oval pods adhere inside the opened calyx.

Psoralea patens (Native verbine) – seen at Standley Chasm

Genus *Erythrina*

These are trees, with large red pea flowers, leaves with 3 leaflets which may be lobed, and pods which are woody and constricted between the seeds.
The name *erythrina* comes from Greek *erythros* meaning *red*. There are 5 species in Australia.

Erythrina vespertilio (Bean tree, Batswing coral tree)

This tree has light balsa-like wood which is used by the Aborigines to make shields and carved dishes. The name *vespertilio* means *a bat* and refers to the shape of the leaflets.

The large red flowers hang on smooth stalks in a cluster which is up to 30 cm long. The flower is a keeled pea. It has a large furled standard 3-4 cm long, and shorter wing and keel petals. There is a long brown calyx. The pods contain large red or brown seeds which the Aborigines use for decorations.

Aborigines at Uluru have recorded that seeds from the bean tree used to be planted beside Ayers Rock in a place where there is a seepage area. The seedlings were harvested when the root was parsnip-size, and the root was roasted and eaten.

Erythrina vespertilio (Bean tree) – leaflet (top) is bat-shaped; flower (below) showing furled standard petal and long brown calyx

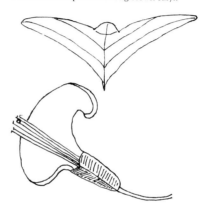

Erythrina vespertilio (Bean tree, Batswing coral tree)

Erythrina vespertilio (Bean tree, Batswing coral tree)

Genus *Vigna*

Vigna lanceolata (Pencil yam)

This pea is a perennial, and has a large taproot which can be baked and eaten. The leaves have 3 leaflets. The yellow flowers are in small clusters, on stems up to 20 cm long. The pods are smooth and slightly curved.

Genus *Glycine*

The name *glycine* comes from the Greek *glykys* meaning *sweet*. Glycines are vine-like pea plants which scramble over other bushes. They have 3 leaflets, short flower spikes and a narrow pod which splits spirally.

Glycine canescens (Silky glycine)

The name *canescens* comes from a Latin word meaning *to become white* and refers to the silky covering of short white hairs. This vine is found climbing all over small bushes and grasses. The stems are slender and each leaf has 3 long narrow pointed leaflets. The flowers are pink, blue or lilac. The pod is about 3 cm x 4 mm and finely haired. The root is woody.

Vigna lanceolata (Pencil yam)

G. falcata

This is a similar plant to *G. canescens*, but it has oval leaflets and a curved pod.

Glycine canescens (Silky glycine)

Geraniaceae (geranium family)

Members of this family are variously called crowfoot, cranebill and storkbill because the fruits have a beak-like appearance (due to long bristles on the fruitlets).

Genus *Erodium* (crowfoot)

Erodium are short-lived herbs with deeply divided leaves. The flowers are on stalks in clusters and are blue, pink or white. The fruit has a long beak. There are 2 introduced *Erodium* species in CA-NT, and 2 native.

Erodium cygnorum (Storkbill, Blue crowfoot)

There are 2 subspecies of *E. cygnorum in* CA-NT – ssp. *glandulosum* and ssp. *cygnorum*.

E. cygnorum ssp. *glandulosum*

This annual shoots prolifically after good autumn or winter rains, and can provide useful stock fodder. The branches spread sideways and upwards to 60 cm. The plant is covered with soft glandular hairs and has much divided ovate leaves up to 5 cm long. The small flowers are in stalked clusters of 2-6 and have blue petals. The individual flower-stalks are up to 4 cm long and are covered with glandular hairs. The calyx has a covering of long glandular hairs and the fruit has a beak which, when mature, splits into five fruitlets, each with a long coiled bristle. These fruitlets can cause injury to sheep. The root is large and fleshy, and used to be cooked and eaten by the Aborigines.

Erodium cygnorum (Storkbill, Blue crowfoot)

E. cygnorum ssp. *cygnorum*

This subspecies is similar, but has non-glandular hairs which are absent on the individual flower-stalks.

E. crinitum (Native crowfoot)

Native crowfoot is very like *E. cygnorum*, but is covered with soft hairs which are not glandular.

Zygophyllaceae

This family includes *Zygophyllum* (twinleaf), *Tribulus* (catshead), and *Nitraria* (Dillon bush).

Genus *Zygophyllum* (twinleaf)

Zygophyllum have hairless two-lobed leaves. The flowers are usually yellow with 3-5 petals, and the fruit is a winged nut or an angled capsule. There are 11 species found in CA-NT. Some have been suspected of causing stock poisoning.

Zygophyllum idiocarpum

This twinleaf is a spreading hairless annual with leaves which have 2 leaflets and a winged stalk. The yellow petals are small, 3-4 mm long. The five-angled capsule is 5-7 mm long.

Zygophyllum idiocarpum (twinleaf)

Genus *Tribulus*

Tribulus are prostrate herbs found in disturbed areas. They have divided leaves, and yellow flowers with 5 petals. The woody fruit capsule may be spiked or winged. There are 7 species in CA-NT and all have similar flowers and leaves. They are distinguished by their fruits. *T. terrestis* (Caltrop) is well known because of its spiky fruits.

Tribulus macrocarpus

This species has a leaf with 12-14 leaflets. The yellow flower is about 1 cm in diameter. The globular fruit has 5 wings, each of which has 2 spines.

Tribulus macrocarpus

Euphorbiaceae

This is a large and important family of shrubs and herbs, which often have milky sap. The small inconspicuous flowers sometimes have no petals. The fruit is a capsule which splits into several fruitlets. Poinsettia is a member of this family, as also are the trees from which rubber is obtained. Many Australian Euphorbiaceae are poisonous to stock, including some species of *Euphorbia* and *Phyllanthus*. *Ricinus communis*, the Castor oil plant, is native to Africa and Asia, but has become naturalised in Australia. It is classified as a noxious weed in the NT as it is very poisonous to both man and animals.

There are 12 genera of Euphorbiaceae found in CA-NT.

Genus *Euphorbia* (caustics)

Euphorbia are herbs or small shrubs which have astringent milky sap. The tiny flowers have no petals and are clustered inside a cup, with the female flower in the centre on a long stalk. The fruit capsule develops on this stalk and has 3 fruitlets. Species of the genus *Euphorbia* are called 'caustics' in the NT, because of the caustic nature of the milky sap. This sap has been used medicinally to treat warts, and also as a component in some medicines. Not all plants called 'caustics' belong to this family.

There are 14 *Euphorbia* species found in CA-NT.

Euphorbia species can be recognised by the small flower cups with stalked fruits, and the milky sap.

Euphorbia drummondii (Caustic weed, Red soldier)

Euphorbia drummondii
(Caustic weed, Red soldier)

Caustic weed is a small prostrate plant which readily springs up after rain. The stems are usually red and the fruits turn red. They look like small helmets. The tiny flowers are clustered in a pink cup and the stalked rounded fruit projects from this. The small leaves, 4-8 mm long, are oval or oblong and hairless.

This was the species whose white sap was mostly used medicinally by Aborigines and early settlers. There are reports of its toxicity to stock, but it does not seem to cause problems when used in mixed forage. Travelling or hungry stock may be susceptible.

E. australis (Hairy caustic weed)

This is similar to *E. drummondii* but it is hairy. It also can be poisonous to stock.

E. tannennsis (Desert spurge, Caustic bush)

This small, erect, hairless shrub is 20-60 cm high. The leaves are narrow, about 7 cm x 7 mm, and drop off early leaving the plant nearly leafless. The stalked fruits can be seen growing out of the flower-cup. This species has the reputation for being very poisonous to stock, but is not usually grazed.

Euphorbia tannensis (Caustic bush) showing fruit 3-6 mm long, flower cup about 3 mm long, male flowers in flower cup

Euphorbia tannensis (Desert spurge, Caustic bush)

Euphorbia tannensis ssp. *eremophila*

Genus *Phyllanthus*

Phyllanthus species have milky sap and fleshy blue-green leaves. The small flowers are in a cup of petal-like tepals; the male flowers are in clusters and the female flowers separate. The fruit is a stalked capsule with 2 fruitlets.

There are 4 *Phyllanthus* species in CA-NT.

Phyllanthus fuernrohrii (Sand spurge)

This is a shrub up to 40 cm high, with smooth fleshy stems, and leaves which have a covering of minute spreading hairs. It can be annual or perennial. The tiny male flowers are in clusters of 3, on short stalks, and the female flowers are separate, with longer stalks.

The flattened globular fruit is 5-6 mm wide. This species is found mainly on sandy plains and has been suspected of poisoning stock.

Genus *Ricinus*

Ricinus communis (Castor oil plant)

This is an introduced plant which is sometimes found growing in disturbed places.

It can be recognised by its palm-shaped, toothed leaves, and bright red spiky fruits. The fruits are extremely poisonous to people and animals. Castor oil can be extracted from the seeds.

Phyllanthus fuernrohrii (Sand spurge)

Sapindaceae

This family includes Whitewood, Rosewood and Hopbush. They grow as trees or shrubs which often have separate male and female flowers, sometimes on separate plants.
The flowers are small and may have petals or be without. The fruits are hard, either lobed or winged.

Genus *Atalaya*

Atalaya mostly have bisexual flowers which are in clusters. The flowers have 5 petals, 8 stamens and a thick style. The fruit separates into winged fruitlets.

Atalaya hemiglauca (Whitewood)

The word *hemiglauca* means *becoming whitish-grey*. Whitewood is a smooth, hairless tree, which grows to 5 m. The trunk usually has flaky grey bark, and the branches are whitish-grey. The divided leaves have 2-6 pairs of long, narrow, leathery leaflets (6-20 x 1-2 cm), which hang downwards.

The bell-shaped white flowers have 5 petals and hang in large clusters. The petals are broad, about 8 x 4 mm in size. The hairy fruit consists of 2 or 3 fruitlets joined together. Each fruitlet is 3-4 cm long, including the large membranous wing.

Atalaya hemiglauca (Whitewood) – winged fruitlets

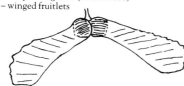

Whitewood is found through most of dry inland Australia. Suckering is frequent and the species copes well with drought and fire. It is an important stock fodder, both palatable and nutritious. There is some evidence of toxicity at times, especially of the suckers and fruits, but cases of poisoning are rare and are far outweighed by the importance of the plant as a topfeed.

Atalaya hemiglauca (Whitewood)

Genus *Heterodendrum*

Heterodendrum oleaefolium (Bullock bush, Rosewood)

This small tree grows to 4 m high. The mature leaves are grey-green, 4-14 cm long, and leathery. The flowers have no petals. The fruits have 2-3 globular segments, each containing one black seed. They have fleshy red stalks, which were eaten by the Aborigines. The plant is moderately nutritious for stock, but can be poisonous at the time of flowering. In the NT, bullock bush is found only in a limited central area surrounding Alice Springs.

Genus *Dodonaea* (hopbush)

Hopbushes are shrubs which are often very sticky. There are usually male and female flowers in clusters on separate bushes. The male flowers have the anthers arranged in a circle, with very short filaments. They are usually red or orange. The female flowers have a small cup, with the style in the centre.

The fruit is a membranous angled capsule which may have 2-6 wings. There are 5 species in CA-NT, and these have differences in leaf and capsule. The fruits of hopbushes look like hops, but they are botanically not related. However, early settlers used them for brewing beer, and they did produce a satisfactory drink.

Dodonaea viscosa ssp. *mucronata* (Sticky hopbush)

Sticky hopbush is widespread in tropical regions and is very variable. Subspecies *mucronata* has a shiny green, spade-shaped leaf, about 2-6 x 1-2 cm, with wavy margins. The fruit capsule is similar to that of several other species; it has 3-4 wings, and the fruitlets are not inflated. The wings are 5 mm wide and the capsule is about 2 cm long.

Dodonaea viscosa ssp. *mucronata* (Sticky hopbush)

Dodonaea viscosa ssp. *mucronata* (Sticky hopbush) – fruiting capsule seen in side elevation (top) and cross section (below)

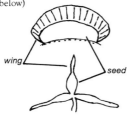

wing

seed

Dodonaea viscosa ssp. *angustissima* (Desert hopbush) male flowers ▶

Dodonaea viscosa ssp. *mucronata* (Sticky hopbush) female flowers

D. viscosa ssp. *angustissima*
(Desert hopbush)

This has a similar, but smaller, capsule. The leaf is long and narrow (4-8 cm x 4-8 mm), with slightly toothed margins.

D. microgyza (Hopbush)

This hopbush has small leaves (less than 1.5 cm long), with 2-6 leaflets. The capsule has 3-4 wings which are 2.5-6 mm wide. It is not inflated.

D. petiolaris (Hopbush)

D. petiolaris has stalked leaves which are hairless and sticky. They are densely covered with glands, and are 3-5 cm long with a pointed end. The capsule is 3 lobed and greatly inflated. The wings are very narrow.

D. coriacea (Hopbush)

This hopbush has wedge-shaped leaves which have no stalks and are only 1.5-2.7 cm long. They are sticky, toothed at the end, and covered with brown glands. The capsule is 3-4 winged, with wings 5 mm wide. It is not inflated.

D. lanceolata (Hopbush)

This hopbush has stalked pointed leaves which are up to 10 cm long. They are hairless, but not sticky. The capsule has 3 wings which are up to 5.5 mm wide.

Stackhousiaceae

Genus *Macgregoria*

Macgregoria racemigera (Snow-flake)

Snow-flake grows as small dense clusters of highly scented white flowers. These develop from a single stem at the base, and reach only 10 cm high and are 10-15 cm in diameter. They appear scattered around in clusters on the bare earth. The fruit is 3-5 nutlets.

Macgregoria racemigera (Snow-flake)

Genus *Stackhousia*

There are several species of *Stackhousia* found in CA-NT. These have small, yellow, tubular flowers, and fruits of various shapes.

Stackhousia megaloptera

This *Stackhousia* is often found on sand-dunes. The plant is a perennial, 25-50 cm high, and has many stems. The leaves are narrow. The small, yellow, tubular flowers are in clusters of 3-6 along long spreading stems. The fruits are hairless, 5-10 mm long, with 3 prominent wings. The name *megaloptera* means *large wing,* and refers to the wings on the fruit.

Stackhousia megaloptera

Rhamnaceae

Genus *Ventilago*

Ventilago viminalis (Supplejack)

This small tree looks rather like Whitewood, although it is from a different family. It characteristically has several intertwining trunks. These are covered by rough, flaky, grey-brown bark. The long narrow leaves are 5-15 cm x 6-12 mm, and hang down. The flowers are small and without petals. The fruit is a globular nut with a leathery wing 2-4 cm long.

Supplejack is found in the southern two-thirds of the NT and adjacent arid regions. It is nutritious and palatable to stock and lopped as topfeed in times of drought.

Ventilago viminalis (Supplejack) tree

Ventilago viminalis (Supplejack) seeds

Malvaceae (hibiscus and mallow family)

Hibiscus are the best known of Malvaceae because of their popularity as garden plants. There are a number of native hibiscus which thrive in the dry inland in spite of their apparent delicacy. *Hibiscus, Radyera* and *Gossypium* (Desert rose) have large flowers – lilac, pink or white, with a dark-red or purple throat spot. *Abutilon* are commonly called mallows. They have yellow flowers. *Sida* have smaller yellow flowers. The name *hibiscus* is derived from an ancient name for Marshmallow, which is a European member of this family. Throughout recorded history Marshmallow has been an important medicinal herb, and is still used today. The mucilaginous gel which is obtained from Marshmallow is present in all family members and it has been used medicinally in Asia as well as in Europe. In Australia both Aborigines and early settlers used the hibiscus family widely. As well as the varied internal and external medicinal uses of the gel – for coughs, colds, dysentery, and dressings – the flowers and buds can be eaten, and the strong inner bark can be used for cord to make fishing lines, nets and bags. In CA, *Lavatera plebeia* (Native hollyhock), and *Abutilon otocarpum* (Keeled mallow), were the main sources of fibre. *Sida rhombifolia* and *S. rohlenae* (both called Paddy's lucerne) were widely used for the medicinal gel and also to obtain fibre. There was even an attempt to cultivate *S. rhombifolia* in India for the copra trade.

In CA-NT, Malvaceae includes *Hibiscus, Radyera, Alyogyne, Gossypium, Lavatera, Malva, Malvastrum, Lawrencia, Abutilon* and *Sida.*

They grow as shrubs or herbs which are often covered with star-shaped hairs, and are rough or bristly to touch.

The trumpet-shaped flower has 5 flaring, overlapping petals and a calyx cup which may have an epicalyx (a second row of leafy segments). The style often has 5 branches (can be 2-10). These may be free, or fused into a club-shaped end. There are many stamens, which are fused in a cuff around the style. The leaves are often palm-shaped or lobed, and toothed. The dry seed capsule is divided into compartments which surround a central axis.

Malvaceae can be divided into groups, according to the epicalyx. The *Hibiscus* group have 8-10 epicalyx segments, *Gossypium* have 3 epicalyx segments and *Sida* and *Abutilon* have no epicalyx.

Seen under magnification, several hairs radiate from one centre and lie flat, making a star-like shape

Genus *Hibiscus*

The *Hibiscus* group also includes *Alyogyne* and *Radyera*. *Hibiscus* has a branched style, with 5 free ends. *Alyogyne* has an undivided style and 8 free epicalyx segments. *Radyera* has an undivided style and 10 clubbed epicalyx segments which form a cup.

There are 10 *Hibiscus* species found in CA-NT, 1 *Radyera*, and 1 *Alyogyne*.

Hibiscus sturtii (Sturt's hibiscus)

This is a small shrub which grows up to 60 cm tall. The epicalyx is fused into a globular cup which surrounds the calyx. The toothed calyx is 8-25 mm long and the epicalyx cup which surrounds it may be toothed or not. There are several varieties. The flowers are trumpet-shaped, lilac, pink or white, usually with a purple or red throat spot. The 5-ended style is surrounded by many stamens. The plant is rough to touch, due to a dense covering of white or grey star-shaped hairs. The leaves vary from oblong to ovate, with toothed edge and pointed end. They are 2-4 cm long.

Hibiscus flower (seen in cross section) showing ovary with 5-ended style and 5 stigmas, and stamens emerging from the cup

Hibiscus – calyx and epicalyx in 2 different species, *H.sturtii* (left) and *H.solanifolia*

Hibiscus sturtii (Sturt's hibiscus)

H. solanifolius (Tomato-leaved hibiscus)

This bush grows 50 cm-1 m high. The name *solanifolius* means *tomato-leaved*. The bush has lobed tomato-like leaves on its lower parts and oblong leaves higher up. The trumpet-like flower is large, 4-5 cm long, and is lilac with a dark purple throat spot. The calyx cup has long pointed lobes, and the epicalyx has 8-10 short thread-like segments. The plant has a dense bristly covering of golden star-shaped hairs.

H. krichauffianus (Velvet-leaf hibiscus)

Velvet-leaf hibiscus is a small velvety shrub with fine soft hairs. The pink or lilac flowers are trumpet-shaped, with petals 2.5-3 cm long. The leaves are toothed, ovate or oblong, and 2-4 cm long. The calyx is about 1 cm long and has pointed lobes. The epicalyx has 6-8 narrow segments united at the base.

Hibiscus solanifolius (Tomato-leaved hibiscus)

H. burtonii (Burton's hibiscus)

This small shrub has bristly star-shaped hairs. The leaves are narrow, oblong and 2-3 cm long. The flower is lilac and trumpet-shaped. The calyx is 1 cm long, with deeply divided lobes. The epicalyx has 8-9 segments which are only 2 mm long.

H. leptocladus

This small shrub has a variable hairy covering. It is found north of Alice Springs and also west of the Olgas. The pink or lilac flowers have a purple throat spot and are smaller than other native hibiscuses. The name *leptocladus* means *slender branches*. The calyx cup is 1 cm long with deeply divided lobes, and the epicalyx has 7-9 small thread-like segments. This is a very variable plant.

Hibiscus krichauffianus (Velvet-leaf hibiscus)

Genus *Alyogyne*

Alyogyne pinoniana (Sand hibiscus)

Alyogyne are only found in Australia. *Alyogyne pinoniana* (Sand hibiscus) is found in the sand-dune country south-west of Alice Springs. It grows in many-stemmed bushes 1-2 m high. The yellow-green foliage is rough to touch because of a dense covering of yellow star-shaped hairs. The leaves are coarsely lobed and 3-4 cm long. The large, trumpet-shaped flowers may be lilac, pink or blue, with a purple throat spot. They tend to furl up at the hottest time of day. The style is undivided, with 5 small stigmas on the end, and the stamens surround the style. The densely hairy calyx is deeply divided and surrounded at the base by 8-10 narrow epicalyx segments.

Alyogyne pinoniana (Sand hibiscus)
flower closed in bright sunlight

Genus *Radyera*

Radyera farragei (Bush hibiscus)

Bush hibiscus grows as a bush 1-2 m high, and is found along water-courses and also by roadsides. It is a long-lived perennial and a good garden plant; an elegant bush with large floppy leaves, and large deep-lilac flowers. It is often called Sturt's desert rose, but this, technically is not correct. Sturt's desert rose can be distinguished because the plant is hairless, and is dotted with black spots.

Bush hibiscus has a large trumpet-shaped flower which is deep-lilac with a dark purple throat spot. The style is undivided with a club-shaped end which has a 5 lobed stigma. The stamens surround the style. The globular fruit sits in the calyx-cup which is surrounded in the lower part by an epicalyx with 10 club-shaped lobes which form a frill. The floppy leaves are

Radyera farragei (Bush hibiscus)

large (10 x 12 cm), palm-shaped and toothed. They are green above and white underneath, due to a dense covering of white hairs. The whole bush is densely covered with star-shaped hairs which make it rough to touch.

Radyera farragei (Bush hibiscus) – flower seen in cross section

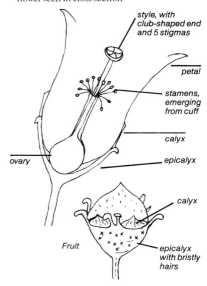

style, with club-shaped end and 5 stigmas

petal

stamens, emerging from cuff

calyx

ovary

epicalyx

calyx

Fruit

epicalyx with bristly hairs

Radyera farragei (Bush hibiscus)

Radyera farragei (Bush hibiscus)

Genus *Gossypium*

Some genera of Malvaceae have an epicalyx with 3 segments. In CA-NT these include *Gossypium, Lavatera, Malva* and *Malvastrum. Gossypium* includes the imported species from which we obtain commercial cotton. The cotton is the seed covering. All *Gossypium* species have seeds which are densely woolly. *Gossypium* are perennial shrubs, with the black-spotting of oil glands on most parts. The epicalyx has 3 segments, which may be narrow, or large and leafy. The large flower has a dark throat spot. The style is undivided, with a bulge at its end and 5 stigmas.

Gossypium sturtianum (Sturt's desert rose)

This is the floral emblem of the NT and is widely planted in the gardens of Alice Springs, including Anzac Hill, the Diarama and Araluen. Sturt's desert rose is found in the bush around Alice Springs and to the south; mainly in rocky gullies, but also on sand plains.

The plants are perennial and live about 10 years. The hibiscus-like flower is a delicate pale lilac, pink, or white, with a red throat spot. The petals are somewhat translucent. The undivided style has a bulge at the end, and stamens surround the style. The fruits are distinctive; 3 large, triangular, black-spotted epicalyx leaves fully enclose the fruit. The bush grows 1-2 m high. The hairless, blue-green leaves are round or ovate, and scented when crushed. The whole plant is hairless, the only Malvaceae of CA-NT to be so. Black-spotting can be seen on most parts of the plant. The seed hairs are flattened.

There are 2 other Desert roses in CA-NT, *G. australe* and *G. bickii,* which are found mostly to the north of Alice Springs.

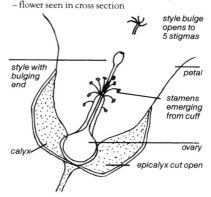

Gossypium sturtianum (Sturt's desert rose) – flower seen in cross section

style bulge opens to 5 stigmas

style with bulging end

petal

stamens emerging from cuff

calyx

ovary

epicalyx cut open

Gossypium sturtianum (Sturt's desert rose)

Both have black-spotting, 3 epicalyx leaves and a flower like Sturt's desert rose. They differ from *G. sturtianum* in that they are both hairy shrubs, both have a calyx with long narrow segments, and the 3 epicalyx leaves are long and narrow and hang away from the calyx.

G. *australe* (Desert rose)

This is a shrub, 1-2 m tall, with a soft silky hairy covering. The flower is usually lilac with a dark purple throat spot. The leaves are elliptic or ovate. The calyx is ribbed and constricted towards the base, and has long narrow pointed lobes. The epicalyx has 3 narrow leaves which hang loose at the base. The seed capsule is covered with soft hairs, and the seed hairs are straight and bristly.

G. *bickii* (Desert rose)

This is a hairy spreading shrub which grows 1 m high. The leaves are elliptic to ovate, or lobed. The flower is pink with a red throat spot. The seed capsule is globular and hairless. The calyx has long narrow lobes, and the epicalyx 3 narrow leaves. The seed hairs are flattened.

Gossypium australe (Desert rose)

Gossypium bickii (Desert rose)

Abutilon and Sida

Abutilon and *Sida* have no epicalyx. In CA, *Abutilon* are commonly called mallows, although that is really the common name for the whole family. Lantern bush is another popular common name. The garden ornamental Chinese lattern is an *Abutilon*. Sidas have no special common name. *Abutilon* and *Sida* in CA-NT have yellow flowers, with those of *Sida* usually being smaller (5-10 mm in diameter). As in the hibiscus flower, the petals overlap and the flower may be like a trumpet or a cup. The calyx supports the flower and then encloses the fruits. The flower has a central column with a many-ended style and a mass of stamens emerging from the stamen-cuff. Sida flowers have a stiff stalk which is usually long and thread-like, and often jointed beneath the flower. The flower-stalk of the abutilon is usually thicker. Leaf shape varies. Sida leaves tend to be narrow-oblong, often serrated and variably hairy. The hairy abutilon leaves are large and rounded, with serrated edges. The base is notched and the end pointed. Most species are perennial, with a strong root sytem. Most are small shrubs or woody herbs. They can be identified by their fruits and seeds.

Genus *Abutilon*

Abutilon leucopetalum (Desert lantern flower)

This small shrub grows about 30 cm high. The densely hairy leaves (2-8 cm long), are round or ovate, and toothed. The calyx is bell-shaped, ribbed, and 14-20 mm long. The yellow trumpet-shaped flower is twice as long as the calyx. The name *leucopetalum* was given because dried specimens had white petals.

Abutilon leucopetalum (Desert lantern flower)

A. *cryptopetalum* (Hill lantern flower)

This small shrub can be much like A. *leucopetalum* in leaf and form, but the leaves are usually narrower and the flower and calyx are much smaller. The calyx is 10 mm long and 10-ribbed. The petals are scarcely longer than the calyx. The name *cryptopetalum* is from *crypto* meaning *hidden*, as the petals tend to be hidden by the calyx. The flower may look like a sida but its stalk is thicker. This plant is usually found near gorges and rocky outcrops.

A. *otocarpum* (Desert Chinese lantern)

This is a small shrub with dense velvety covering, and it often flowers when it is about 25 cm tall. Desert Chinese lantern is usually first noticed because of the calyx, which has 5 keels which are so prominent that they are almost winged. The calyx is about 12 mm long; the fruit has a depressed centre and ear-shaped fruitlets. The name *otocarpum* means *ear fruits*. Aborigines used the strong fibre from the underbark to make fishing lines, bags and string. Desert Chinese lantern has a strong perennial rootstock and shoots up quickly after rain. It is widespread in and around Alice Springs, at Rainbow Valley, and in other sandy places.

Abutilon otocarpum (Desert Chinese lantern) – keeled fruiting capsule

Abutilon cryptopetalum (Hill lantern flower)

Abutilon otocarpum (Desert chinese lantern)

A. fraseri (Dwarf lantern flower)

Dwarf lantern flower can be mistaken for a sida because it is a small plant with small yellow flowers. Identifying points are: a square-shaped calyx, fruits with 10 fruitlets and a depressed centre, and flowers on stout hairy stalks. Long straight hairs and short star-shaped hairs are seen together on the stems. Each fruitlet has 2 downy seeds. The yellow flower has petals twice as long as the calyx, which is about 7 mm long. The plant grows in rocky areas, as a scrambler or a small upright plant 20-40 cm high.

A. macrum, A. halophilum and A. lepidum are also found in CA-NT.

Abutilon fraseri (Dwarf lantern flower)

Sida rohlenae (Shrub sida) – seed with 2 sharp spines

3 mm

Genus *Sida*

Sida rohlenae (Shrub sida)

Shrub sida is very similar to S. rhombifolia (Paddy's lucerne). It is a strong woody small shrub 30-50 cm high, often found in flood-out areas or disturbed ground, and a frequent weed of gardens and footpaths. The leaves are finely haired, narrow, oblong and toothed. The flowers are small (about 1 cm in diameter), yellow and hibiscus-shaped, with sida characteristics.

Like Paddy's lucerne, Shrub sida can be distinguished from other sidas by the calyx, which has 10 strongly marked ribs, and the fruitlets, which each have 2 hard, sharp spikes. These spikes can be dangerous to fowls if the plant is fed to them. A jelly can be made from a decoction of the leaves and roots. This was used medicinally by the Aborigines and early settlers. Aborigines also used the fibrous underbark for cord and twine.

Sida rohlenae (Shrub sida)

Sida filiformis (Fine sida)

S. *filiformis* (Fine sida)

Fine sida is a low spreading perennial with long trailing stems. The densely hairy toothed leaves have short stalks. The cup-like yellow flowers have petals 5-6 mm long and have long thread-like stalks which are jointed below the flower. The hairy calyx is 2-5 mm long, and the fruit is 4 mm in diameter with 5-6 wrinkled fruitlets. It is found on rocky hillsides. The name *filiformis* means *thread-like*.

S. *fibulifera* (Silver sida or Pin sida)

This species is a woody perennial with spreading or erect stems to 40 cm long. The toothed leaves are variably hairy. The small yellow flowers are solitary or in clusters, on thread-like stalks up to 2 cm long. The petals are about 4 mm long.

The calyx is 3-4 mm shorter than the fruit, so the bulging fruit on its stalk looks like a hatpin.

Sida fibulifera (Silver sida or Pin sida)

S. petrophila (Rock sida)

The name *petrophila* means *rock-lover*. This low shrub grows in and near rocks. The densely hairy grey-green leaves are narrow-oblong to arrow-shaped, and coarsely toothed. The small yellow flowers have long jointed thread-like stalks. The calyx enlarges in fruiting to about 10 mm long, and the fruit has a central protuberance.

Sida petrophila (Rock sida)

S. trichopoda (High sida)

This species is an erect shrub which grows to 50 cm high. The leaves are 1-3 cm long. They are ovate or narrow-oblong, usually with toothed edges, and are only sparsely hairy. The flowers have long thread-like stalks jointed just below the flower. The hairy fruit is 5-7 mm in diameter, usually with a depressed centre, but may be knobbed. There are 7-8 fruitlets. This species is widespread and has several forms. The name *trichopoda* means *hair foot*, which refers to the thread-like stalk of the flowers.

Sida trichopoda (High sida)

S. platycalyx (Lifesaver burr)

Lifesaver burr is a low-growing perennial which has 2 forms: one is erect and the other prostrate. The yellow hibiscus-shaped flower is larger than usual for sida, up to 2 cm in diameter, and the flower-stalk is thicker than usual. The seed-capsule is also large, up to 2.5 cm in diameter. It is round and flattened, and looks like a lifesaver. The capsule has a papery covering and about 20 fruitlets which join in the centre. They have large stiff spines on their backs. The name *platycalyx* means *flattened calyx*.

S. cryphiopetala (Hill sida or Rusty sida)

This straggly erect shrub grows to 2 m tall and is found in rocky gorges. It can be seen at Standley Chasm and at the Olgas. The plant, which is often rust coloured, has a thick velvety covering of star-shaped hairs. The narrow-ovate leaves are toothed. The small yellow flowers are on thread-like stalks, which are jointed below the flower. The calyx looks woolly, being almost hidden in its hairy covering. The conical fruits have 5 fruitlets.

Sida platycalyx (Lifesaver burr)

There are 10 other species of sida found in CA-NT. Many are confusingly similar. Although they are mostly small plants they are important, because, like all perennials, they have the valuable ability to hold the soil.

Sida cryphiopetala (Hill sida or Rusty sida)

Sterculiaceae (kurrajong family)

This family includes the cocoa tree of South America and the cola tree from Africa. In CA-NT it includes *Brachychiton, Melhania, Rulingia* and *Keraudrenia,* and several other genera.

Genus *Brachychiton* (kurrajongs)

These are trees which have large leaves. The flowers have no petals, but are formed by a bell-shaped calyx cup. Male and female flowers are separate. The woody fruit capsules hang in clusters and the seeds are embedded in a honeycomb-like material which holds them with coarse hairs.

There are 12 species which are all Australian and these include the Illawarra flame tree, the kurrajong of eastern Australia and the bottle-tree. Kurrajongs – *Brachychiton populneus* from the Eastern States, *B. gregorii* (Desert kurrajong), and hybrids – are widely planted as street trees in Alice Springs.

B. gregorii (Desert kurrajong)

This tree grows to 8 m high. The large leaves are shiny and hairless, with 3-5 graceful lobes. The cream bell-shaped flowers are large, 2 cm long, and hang in clusters. This kurrajong is found scattered through the desert areas of CA-NT, SA and WA. It has always been of great value to the Aborigines, early settlers and explorers. Water can be obtained from the roots, and rope and string can be made from the bark. The tree is widely used for cattle fodder and lopped when needed. The Aborigines roasted the seeds and ate them whole, or ground them to make cakes. They also ate the taproot of seedlings. They found seeds and seedlings – where crows dropped them – beside the inland waterholes. Early explorers made a 'coffee' from the ground-up seeds.

Brachychiton gregorii (Desert kurrajong)

Genus *Melhania*

Melhania oblongifolia (Velvet hibiscus)

Melhania oblongifolia is the only *Melhania* found in CA-NT. It looks like a sida or abutilon, but is not related and although called 'Velvet hibiscus', it is not a hibiscus. The yellow flower has petals about 12 mm long. The style has 5 branches. There are only 5 stamens and 5 petal-like staminodes. The flower-stalk is jointed. The seed capsule has a brown papery cap. The toothed oblong leaves are densely covered with star-shaped hairs. Like all in this family, the leaves are darker on the upper surface and paler underneath.

Melhania oblongifolia (Velvet hibiscus)

Genus *Rulingia*

Rulingia species are low shrubs with a dense covering of star-shaped hairs. The leaves are green above and paler beneath. The small flowers are in clusters and the small petals are inside the calyx. The fruiting capsule is covered with star-shaped hairs.

Rulingia loxophylla

The name *loxophylla* means *oblique leaves*. The leaves are oval with a toothed edge. They are shiny dark-green above and white beneath where there is a dense hairy covering. The pale green calyx is 2-4 mm long, with the smaller yellow petals inside. The densely hairy fruit is about 3 mm wide, and it has 5 longitudinal ridges. The plants are low and spreading, 20-30 cm high, and are found in deep sand.

R. rotundifolia

The word *rotundifolia* means *round-leaves*. The leaves are oval to oblong with wavy margins, the flowers 3-4 mm in diameter, and the globular hairy fruit 15-20 mm in diameter. This species is found in rocky places.

R. magniflora

The name *magniflora* means *big flowers*. The calyx is pink and petal-like, and 10-12 mm long. The shorter petals are inside. The hairy fruit is 6 mm in diameter. This plant is found in rocky areas.

Rulingia loxophylla

Genus *Keraudrenia*

These are shrubs which have flowers
without petals although the large
brightly-coloured sepals of the calyx
look like petals. The flowers are
bisexual.

Keraudrenia integrifolia

K. integrifolia grow as shrubs 40-50 cm
high, and have a rusty-coloured hairy
covering. The flowers have purple-blue
sepals 8 mm long, which fade as the
fruits develop. The fruit is pale-green,
globular, 1 cm in diameter, and densely
covered with soft hairs. It does not
readily separate into fruitlets. The leaves
are oblong and 2-3 cm long. They are
green above and white beneath. The
name *integrifolia* means *whole leaf* and
indicates that the leaves are not lobed.

Keraudrenia integrifolia

Keraudrenia integrifolia

132

K. nephrosperma

This species is found in sandy soils or rocky areas. It is very similar to *K. integrifolia*. The sepals can be rose-pink, but may be purple or white. The principal difference is that the fruits separate into fruitlets, usually 4. These are somewhat kidney-shaped and densely hairy. The name *nephrosperma* means *kidney seed*.

Keraudrenia nephrosperma

Violaceae (violet family)

Genus *Hybanthus*

Hybanthus are perennials. They have an irregular flower with the large lower petal spade-shaped and pouched at the base. The 4 upper petals are very small. The seeds are in a capsule.

Hybanthus aurantiacus (Orange spade flower)

The name *aurantiacus* means *orange-coloured*. *H. aurantiacus* is a golden-orange spade-flower, with the large lower petal 7-15 mm long and the smaller petals 3-5 mm. The hairless leaves are 4 cm long; flat, narrow and toothed. The plant grows about 30-40 cm high.

H. enneaspermus (Blue spade flower)

This is found to the north of Alice Springs. The flowers are blue. The seeds are ribbed.

Hybanthus aurantiacus (Orange spade flower)

Frankeniaceae (sea-heath family)

Sea-heaths are dwarf shrubs or herbs which are salt-tolerant, and often have jointed stems. The leaves are opposite, with a sheath around the base of the leaf and stem. They are dotted with salt-glands and oil-glands plugged with salt. There is also a crusting of salt on the foliage. The flowers have a ridged tubular calyx and 4-6 petals. The fruit is a small capsule enclosed in the calyx.

Frankenia cordata (Sea-heath)

Genus *Frankenia*

This is the only genus of this family occurring in Australia. There are about 50 species, mostly in dry regions, and 12 in CA-NT.

The flowers often have a whorl of leaf-like bracts at their base. The petals are pink or lilac, sometimes white. They are usually wedge-shaped, fluted, and finely toothed at the summit.

Frankenia cordata (Sea-heath)

F. cordata is a low ground-hugging shrub which is found near the edges of salt-lakes and clay-pans. It can be seen at Rainbow Valley. It is a perennial with a woody taproot, and forms hummocks by holding the sand around its root-system. The plant has minute bristles when young, but becomes hairless as it matures. The leaves are oblong to ovate with a notched base and rolled edges. They are 4-8 mm long. The upper surface is hairless and salt-encrusted. Underneath, the leaf is finely haired. The flower has a cylindrical bristly calyx, petals about 1 cm long, and a whorl of bracts around the base.

Frankenia cordata (Sea-heath)

Cucurbitaceae (melon family)

This family includes melons, pumpkin and cucumber. They grow as vines which either spread on the ground or climb using tendrils. The leaves are lobed and usually large. There are separate male and female yellow flowers. The fruit is melon-like, with the seeds embedded in pith or pulp. Several of the species in CA-NT are called Paddy melon. Most are introduced, but some species are native.

Genus *Citrullus*

Citrullus colocynthus (Paddy melon, Colocynth melon)

This species is a relation of the water-melon, and is native to Asia and the Mediterranean. It is a ground-spreading perennial with lobed hairy leaves and yellow flowers. The melon-like fruit is round, 5-12 cm in diameter, and green with white mottling. It is extremely bitter and poisonous, and has been used for the extraction of colocynth, which is a strong purge.

Citrullus colocynthus (Paddy melon, Colocynth melon)

Citrullus lanatus (Wild melon, Camel melon, Bitter or Bastard melon)

This ground-creeping plant is native to southern Africa. The leaves are deeply lobed and hairy, the flowers yellow. The melon fruit is round or oblong, 6-15 cm long and green with white mottling. It is the wild form of the cultivated watermelon.

Citrullus lanatus (Wild melon, Camel melon, Bitter or Bastard melon)

Genus *Cucumis*

Cucumis myriocarpus (Paddy melon)

Cucumis is the genus from which we get cucumbers. *C. myriocarpus*, which is called 'Paddy melon', is native to South Africa. It differs from *Citrullus* in the flowers and the fruit. The fruit is round, 2-2.5 cm in diameter, with soft bristles. It is first a striped green, but turns yellow.

C. melo ssp. *agrestis* (Ulcardo melon)

This is native to CA-NT and also tropical Asia and Africa. The fruit is oblong, 1.5-4 cm long, and greenish. Like all other bush melons, the flesh is very bitter.

Cucumis myriocarpus (Paddy melon)

136

Genus *Mukia*

Mukia maderaspatana (Snake vine)

Snake vine is another member of the melon family native to CA-NT. It is a vine, which climbs over the ground or across plants. The leaves are toothed with 3 lobes, and are 2-7 cm long. There are male and female yellow flowers. The small melon-like fruits are about 1 cm in diameter and are red when ripe. They are not edible. It is found also in the tropics of Australia, Africa and Asia.

Mukia maderaspatana (Snake vine)

Myrtaceae (myrtle family)

This family includes eucalypts, bottlebrush, teatrees, paperbarks and myrtles. The leathery leaves are densely packed with oil-glands which can be seen if the leaf is held against the sun. The leaves are undivided, and in some genera (for example *Thryptomene*), are very small. The flower has 5 sepals and 5 petals which in *Eucalyptus* are formed into a cap. The stamens are usually many, but there are only 5 in *Thryptomene* and 5 or 10 in *Micromyrtus*. They are mounted on a ring at the top of the flower-cup, and are often much longer than the rest of the flower. In most genera the style is short. The fruit is usually a capsule which opens at the top. In a few genera it is a nutlet or berry (eg. lilly-pilly). Eucalypts and teatrees have been widely planted overseas; as ornamentals, for wind-breaks, for the wood, and for their aromatic oils.

Genus *Eucalyptus*

Eucalyptus species secrete a resinous gum. They can grow as trees, shrubs or mallees.

A mallee is a bushy tree which has many trunks arising from a lignotuber, which is a swelling situated at the base of the stem, and from which new growth can develop. A mallee is a type of growth rather than a particular species, but there are some species which are usually seen as mallees. Mallee growth occurs in areas where the soil is poor.

Eucalyptus trees have bark which vary from species to species, and they are sometimes grouped according to bark characteristics. The smooth barked species are called gums. Trees with fibrous bark are called boxes. Stringy-barks have bark which peels in strings, and bloodwoods have tessellated (pavement-like) bark. Grouping by barks does not necessarily group botanically related species together.

The leaves of *Eucalyptus* are different at different ages of the plant. Leaves of the young tree may be hairy, are mostly opposite, and have a different shape from leaves of the mature tree. The adult leaves are hairless, leathery, sometimes opposite but often alternate and usually with stalks. They are nerved with a strong mid-vein, a marginal vein, and veins joining these in a feather-like manner. Some species retain juvenile foliage as adults.

The flower is in a woody cup which has a ring at the top on which the operculum or cap sits. This cap is made up of the sepals and petals, and drops when flowering occurs. The short style is in the centre of the flower, and the long stamens arise from a ring at the top of the cup. The flowers are in clusters.

Identification of *Eucalyptus* species may be difficult even for professionals, as there are a large number of species, and much hybridisation and natural variation. For identification one needs to collect a branch with gumnuts, and make note of the form and the bark of the tree. In national parks where specimens cannot be taken, a drawing with measurements will suffice. Note the shape and size of gumnut and cap, the valves and whether they protrude, the number of gumnuts to a cluster, and the length of their stalks.

Eucalypts are used for their wood, and also for their aromatic oils. The oils used to be extracted in stills in the bush, and this is still done in some places. The nature of the oil varies in different species. It is used in pharmaceuticals and toiletries, and was widely used as a cleaning agent. Dyes can be obtained from eucalyptus leaves and bark. Some eucalypts (such as river red gum and ghost gum) are useful fodder trees, but are not very nourishing. Many species, including River red gum and blood-woods, produce a gum called kino, which was exported for use in medicinal products. The early settlers used eucalyptus bark as a building material, and the Aborigines made bark canoes, bark dishes and shields. They also obtained water from the roots of mallees and coolibah. They ate witchetty grubs from under the bark of some species, grubs from bloodwood apples, and white lerp from gumleaf surfaces (which the Aboriginal children call 'lolly'). Coolibah bark was used for poultices for snakebite. The wet bark forms a firm splint as it dries. The leaves of other eucalypts were used to make poultices and lotions for sore eyes. Eucalyptus bark has many uses as a fibre and in rope making. River red gum and Bloodwood – from which bees can obtain plentiful nectar and pollen – are considered to be good honey trees.

There are over 550 species found in Australia, and over 30 in CA-NT.

Gum (smooth-barked eucalypt)

Eucalyptus papuana (Ghost gum)

These trees grow 5-15 m high, with a spreading crown and drooping branchlets. The bark is smooth and powdery-white. When mature it may lose its whiteness from time to time. The adult leaves are large: 5-18 x 1.2-4.5 cm. The gumnuts are in clusters of 7-11, with short stalks. They are cylindrical, 3-6 mm wide, with the valves inside. Ghost gums are found growing in open sandy country and in rocky areas, where they often seem to be growing out of the rock. The leaves often hang down in long green clusters.

Eucalyptus papuana (Ghost gum)

E. camaldulensis (River red gum)

This was named after some gardens in Italy. It is the most widespread eucalypt in Australia. It is also the most widely planted overseas, used for its wood and oils. It was an important source of food for the Aborigines who ate the ground-up seeds, obtained grubs from under the bark, and lerp (a sugary substance) from the leaves. The trees are large, growing up to 45 m. The bark is smooth, white and grey with red patches, and flakes off from time to time. The adult leaves are narrow, 6-30 x 1-2 cm. The gumnuts are found in stalked clusters of 7-11 with pointed caps in the bud. They are usually 5-8 mm wide, with stalks 5-12 mm long. The valves are protruding.

Eucalyptus camaldulensis (River red gum)

E. gongylocarpa (Marble gum)

This is found westwards in the sand-dune and salt-lake country. The bark is marble-coloured. The leaves are opposite each other. The flowers are in clusters of 4-9 and the valves are inside the gumnut cup.

There are 3 other small gums in CA-NT to the north of Alice Springs. All have grey, white or cream bark.

E. aspera (Rough-leafed gum)

This species is a small tree with smooth grey or white bark, and often has rough tessellated bark at the base. It has rough leaves and stems. The leaves are usually opposite, unstalked, and oblong, ovate or rounded.

Buds and fruits of some *Eucalyptus* species

Eucalyptus papuana   gumnut 5-6 mm long
3-6 mm wide

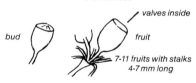

Eucalyptus camaldulensis   gumnut 5-8 x 5-8 mm

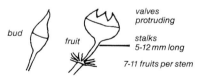

Eucalyptus microtheca   gumnut only 2-3 mm wide,
3-5 mm long

E. brevifolia (Snappy gum)

This is a small crooked tree with brittle branches. The flower clusters are without stalks. The gumnut valves protrude.

Eucalyptus brevifolia (Snappy gum)

E. leucophloia (Snappy gum)

This is very similar to *E. brevifolia*, but flower clusters are stalked. The gumnut valves protrude.

Box (flaky fibrous-barked eucalypts)

È. microtheca (Coolibah tree)

This straggly tree is called *microtheca* because of the *small fruits*. It usually has tough fibrous grey bark. However, the bark may be partly smooth, and the tree is then called a gum coolibah. In the north coolibahs can be found with completely smooth white bark.

Coolibahs are found along watercourses and in swampy areas. The flowers are in clusters of 3-7 and are stalked. The fruits are small, only 2-3 mm wide, and the valves are at (or just above) the gumnut rim. Coolibahs were useful to the Aborigines: the seed as food, grubs from the trunk and lerp from the leaves. They also used the bark medicinally, and obtained water from the roots.

Eucalyptus microtheca (Coolibah tree)

E. intertexta (Gum coolibah)

In this species the upper bark is smooth and the lower bark is box-like. The flowers are in clusters of 4-7, and stalked. The gumnut is 6-8 mm in diameter and has valves at or below the rim.

This tree is found in salty swamp areas and can be seen in the coolibah swamp on the east side of Alice Springs. It can also extend up the rocky ranges where it becomes a mallee.

Eucalyptus intertexta (Gum coolibah)

E. pruinosa (Silver box)

This species can be a tree, a mallee or a shrub. It has a whitish waxy substance on the leaves, buds and fruit. The name *pruinosa* means *covered with a whitish bloom*. Silver box has rough grey bark and opposite leaves. The flowers are in clusters of 3-6, and have stalked gumnuts 6-8 mm wide with valves barely showing. It is found in northern CA-NT and across the Barkly Tablelands.

E. thozetiana (Thozet's box)

This species is found in south-east Queensland and the eastern MacDonnell Ranges, especially on The Gardens station. The tree has smooth bark, which is often striped pink and grey. The flowers are in clusters of 3-8 which are stalked, and the gumnuts are 3-5 mm wide with the valves inside.

Bloodwood (tessellated bark)

Tessellated means 'marked in a pavement pattern of small squares'. Bloodwoods have red wood and large fruits.

E. terminalis (Bloodwood)

This species is a tree with red or grey tessellated bark. The flowers are in clusters of 3-7 and have large pink stalked gumnuts, 2-2.5 cm wide, with the valves inside.

E. setosa (Rough-leafed bloodwood)

This species is found in north CA-NT. The unstalked leaves are opposite and have a rough surface. The flower clusters are 2-3, with bristly stalks. The stalked gumnuts are 2 cm wide, and the valves are inside.

Eucalyptus terminalis (Bloodwood)

Eucalyptus terminalis (Bloodwood) flowers

Mallees (eucalypts which regularly grow as a mallee)

There are many mallees found in CA-NT.

E. gamophylla (Blue mallee)

The bark of the Blue mallee is smooth, often whitish. The blue-green leaves are mostly rounded and joined in pairs, encircling the stem. The flowers, in clusters of 3-7, produce gumnuts 5-7 mm wide with valves at or below the rim. This mallee is found south of Alice Springs. The seeds were used as an Aboriginal food.

Eucalyptus gamophylla (Blue mallee)

Eucalyptus gamophylla (Blue mallee)

E. socialis (Red mallee)

Red mallee is named for the red colour of its smaller branches. The bark is rough at the base and smoother above. The leaves are alternate. The flowers are in clusters of 3-12 with long pointed caps. The gumnuts have protruding valves, and are on stalks. This species is widespread in southern CA-NT, and is used for fencing and firewood. The Aborigines obtained honey from the flowers and water from the roots.

E. pachyphylla (Red-bud mallee)

This species is very similar to E. sessilis, but has stalked flowers in clusters of 3. The buds have pointed caps. The ribbed gumnuts are 12-15 mm wide, with protruding valves. This mallee is found in deep red sand to the north of Alice Springs.

Eucalyptus socialis (Red mallee)

E. sessilis (Finke River mallee)

E. sessilis is found in the western MacDonnell Ranges and was first found at the Finke River. It is called sessilis because the gumnuts have no stalks. The flowers are in clusters of 3-7, and the gumnuts are 18 mm wide with protruding valves.

E. oxymitra (Sharp-capped mallee)

This species has a very sharply pointed cap on the bud. The word oxymitra means sharp-capped. (Some other eucalypts also have sharply pointed caps. These include E. socialis and E. pachyphylla.) The flowers of E. oxymitra are in clusters of 3-7. The gumnuts have short stalks and are 10-15 mm wide, with protruding valves. This mallee can be found in the Common near Alice Springs, and in the south-west of the NT.

Genus Callistemon (bottlebrush)

Bottlebrushes have alternate flat leaves and flowers in dense spikes. There is a flower cup with sepals and small petals. The stamens are numerous and much longer than the sepals and petals. The fruit is a woody gumnut which stays on the tree. Bottlebrushes are native only to Australia.

Callistemon pauciflorus (Desert bottlebrush)

This is a bush or small tree with flat narrow drooping leaves which are closely dotted with oil glands. The flower spikes are generally only 1-2 cm long. The sepals are round with fringed edges and the smaller petals (4 mm long) are cupped. The stamens are pale red, and 10-13 mm long, Desert bottlebrush is found in the rocky gorges of the central mountains of CA-NT.

Callistemon pauciflorus (Desert bottlebrush)

Genus Melaleuca (teatrees and paperbarks)

The common name 'teatree' arose because the early settlers used the leaves to make tea. The spelling teatree is correct, not titree. Tea was also made from *Leptospermum*, another teatree of coastal regions. It also belongs to this family. Paperbarks are species of *Melaleuca* which grow as trees. Their papery bark can be pulled off in wide strips, and it has many uses. Like eucalypts, *Melaleuca* flowers are in cups which develop into a persistent woody fruit or gumnut. The petals are small, about 1-2 mm long. The stamens are in 5 bundles and are 2-6 times as long as the petals.

There are over 100 species which are mostly native to Australia, and about 10 in CA-NT.

Melaleuca glomerata (Inland teatree)

This is one of the most widespread inland teatrees, and is found in Queensland, SA, NT and WA. It grows as a shrub up to 3 m high, with white papery bark. The young branchlets and leaves are finely-haired, making the tree look silvery against the sun. The leaves are alternate, narrow and pointed (1.5 cm x 2 mm). The flower-heads are globular, 1 cm wide, and stalked. The pale yellow stamens are 2-4 mm long. After flowering, the gumnuts can be seen in globular clusters.

Inland teatree is found in sand in low-lying areas – especially around clay-pans, near salt-lakes, and along dry creek-beds.

Melaleuca glomerata (Inland teatree)

Melaleuca glomerata (Inland teatree)

M. *bracteata* (Black teatree)

Black teatree is found in all mainland states except Victoria. It grows along dry creek-beds. The bark is grey. The leaves are short (3-12 mm long), narrow and pointed, and usually finely haired. New growth looks silvery against the light because it is finely haired. The leaves are crowded along the stem. The flowers are in spikes 5-15 cm long, and the creamy stamens are 5 mm long. The gumnuts are 2-3 mm long.

M. *linophylla* (teatree)

This teatree is found from CA-NT westwards into WA. The name *linophylla* means *thread leaves*. The leaves are alternate and very narrow, up to 4.5 cm x 2 mm. The flower spikes are 2-6 cm long, the white stamens 2-3 mm long, and the gumnuts 1-2 mm long.

M. *linariifolia* var. *trichostachya*

This shrubby teatree has papery bark and can grow as a tree. It is found in creek-beds and can be seen in the Finke River at Palm Valley and at Hugh Gorge. The leaves are opposite each other. They are 1-3 cm long, narrow and pointed. Fine hairs make the young growth look silvery. The cream flowers are in loose spikes 2-3 cm long. The 5 bundles of stamens can be clearly seen. They are 3-7 mm long. The gumnuts are 2-3 mm long, with valves protruding.

Melaleuca linariifolia var. *trichostachya*

M. dissitiflora

This teatree grows to the north of Alice Springs. It may grow as a shrub or as a small paperbark tree. The leaves are alternate, straight, narrow and pointed. The flowers are in loose spikes 2-6 cm long. The stamens are 6-7 mm long. The gumnut is urn-shaped, 3 mm long.

Melaleuca dissitiflora (paperbark)

Melaleuca dissitiflora flowers, with urn-shaped gumnuts

Genus *Calytrix* (Fringe myrtle)

Fringe myrtles have a narrow calyx cup about 1 cm long. The stamens are as long as the petals, and the sepals each have 1 long hair-like bristle. The name *calytrix* comes from Greek words meaning *cup* and *hair,* and refers to the long bristles on the ends of the sepals. The leaves are less than 1 cm long.

Calytrix longiflora (Desert fringe myrtle)

This is a low shrub often found on sand-dunes. The crowded thick over-lapping leaves are only 2-3 mm long. The plant is hairless. The pink flowers are in clusters. The large pink sepals are pointed and each ends in a bristle 1 cm long. The pointed pink petals are 8 mm long, and there are many deeper pink stamens the same length as the petals. After flowering the decorative calyx remains on the plant. This is the only *Calytrix* in CA-NT.

Calytrix longiflora (Desert fringe myrtle)

Genus *Thryptomene*

In Greek the word *thryptomene* means *made small*. These plants are shrubs which are always small. The small leaves overlap each other. The small flowers have 5 small petals with a stamen between each petal.

Thryptomene maisonneuvii (Desert heath myrtle)

Thryptomene maisonneuvii (Desert heath myrtle)

This small shrub is found covering wide areas, especially on sand-dunes. The small thick overlapping leaves have no stalks and neither do the small flowers. The pink or white flowers have small round petals with 5 short stamens between the petals. The flowers are only 2 mm in diameter. The fruit develops inside the woody calyx-cup. *T. wittweri* is a similar shrub found in rocky gullies.

Genus *Micromyrtus*

This name comes from Greek words meaning *small myrtle*.

Micromyrtus flaviflora (Yellow heath myrtle)

Yellow heath myrtle is a small shrub found on sand plains and dunes. The small leaves, 2-4 mm long, are paired. The flowers have 5 small rounded petals with frilled edges and 5 stamens. The petals are yellow, turning red. The fruit develops inside the small urn-shaped calyx-cup.

Micromyrtus flaviflora (Yellow heath myrtle)

Apiaceae (parsnip family)

previously Umbelliferae

This is the family from which we get many of the vegetables we eat: carrot, parsnip, parsley and celery; and the spices: carraway, coriander and dill.

Genus *Trachymene* (parsnip)

Trachymene glaucifolia (Wild parsnip)

Wild parsnip has much divided hairless leaves which are mostly at the base of the plant. The flower heads consist of many small white or lilac flowers clustered together. The heads are 1.7-3 cm wide. Wild parsnip was considered poisonous, but tests have not proved positive.

There are several other species of *Trachymene* in CA-NT.

Trachymene glauciflora (Wild parsnip)

Genus *Daucus* (carrot)

Daucus glochidiatus (Australian carrot)

This is the only species of *Daucus* found in Australia. It is widespread, and is eaten by stock. It is a small much-branched erect plant, with leaves like a carrot and small flowers in groups of 1-6 on unequal stalks at the ends of stems. The seeds are in small burrs which can be troublesome.

Genus *Hydrocotyle* (parsley)

Hydrocotyle trachycarpa (Wild parsley)

Wild parsley is a small herb with parsley-like leaves. It is found in moist rocky places.

Genus *Actinotus* (flannel flower)

Actinotus schwarzii (Flannel flower)

This flannel flower of CA-NT is found only in rather inaccessible places on the rock-faces of the mountain ranges. The small flowers are clustered closely to make the centre of a daisy-like flower head. This centre is surrounded by 10 soft white petal-like bracts which look like flannel. The whole flower head is large, up to 7 cm in diameter. The leaves are divided.

Apocynaceae

Genus *Carissa*

Carissa lanceolata (Conkleberry or Conkerberry)

This is a much-branched spiny shrub 1-2 m high. The small white tubular flowers are fragrant. The leaves are narrow and about 2 cm long. The fruit is an oval red berry which becomes black when ripe. It is very tasty, and is an Aboriginal food. The shrub is widespread in NT mainly north of Alice Springs. It is grazed by cattle.

Carissa lanceolata (Conkleberry or Conkerberry)

Carissa lanceolata (Conkleberry or Conkerberry)

Asclepiadaceae

These are perennial shrubs or climbers which usually have white milky sap. Some are poisonous but others have edible fruits. They include Caustic vine, Bush banana, Bush bean and the Desert cynanchum (Native pear). The Hoya is a cultivated member of this family.

Genus *Sarcostemma*

Sarcostemma australe (Caustic vine)

This shrub grows with straggly erect branches which have no leaves. The cylindrical branches are jointed and hairless, pale-green, and have milky sap. The cream waxy star-shaped flowers are in small clusters. The fruit is a cylindrical pod with pointed ends and seeds which have a tuft of silky hairs. These plants are not usually grazed, but can be poisonous to stock.

Sarcostemma australe (Caustic vine)

Sarcostemma australe (Caustic vine)

Genus *Leichhardtia*

Leichhardtia australis (Bush banana, Doubah, Native pear)

This vine can be found clambering on bushes and trees. The thick narrow leaves have very short stalks. The flowers are cream, and about 6-8 mm long. The fruiting pod is pear-shaped (4-9.5 x 3 cm), and hairy. The seeds have a tuft of silky hairs. This fruit was an important Aboriginal food. The pods are roasted and eaten when young.

Genus *Rhyncharrhena*

Rhyncharrhena linearis (Bush bean)

In CA-NT this plant is called 'Bush bean'. It is a vine which twines up other bushes. The leaves are narrow and the plant is hairless. The greenish-yellow flowers are 4-7 mm long. The fruit is a long narrow cylindrical pod, 8-22 cm long, with pointed ends.The seeds have a silky tuft. The pods were eaten by the Aborigines.

Rhyncharrhena linearis (Bush bean)

Leichhardtia australis (Bush banana, Doubah, Native pear)

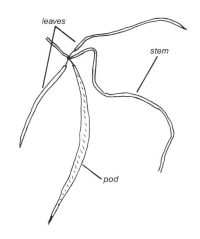

leaves

stem

pod

Genus *Cynanchum*

Cynanchum floribundum (Native pear, Desert cynanchum)

Native pear is found on sand-dunes, often in association with *Zygochloa paradoxa* (Cane grass). It is a twining shrub about 1 m high, and has heart-shaped pointed leaves which are 3-9 cm long. The flowers are about 1 cm long, with a small calyx, and creamy-white petals which are purple-green below. The seed-pod is 3-5 cm long, angled, and tapers to a point. The seeds each have a long tuft of hair. The Aborigines used the inner bark to make string. They also roasted and ate the fruit before it ripened.

Rubiaceae

Genus *Canthium*

Canthium latifolium (Native currant)

Native currant is a hairless shrub or small tree which grows to 4 m high. It can be recognized by its wide lime-green leaves (10 x 3.5 cm). The name *latifolium* means *wide leaf*. The leaves are leathery.

The white flowers are in short-stalked clusters at the leaf-stem angle. The currant-like fruits are black and juicy. They are a prized Aboriginal food. There are other species of Native currant found in CA-NT. They have differences in leaf shape.

Canthium latifolium (Native currant)

Convolvulaceae
(Convolvulus family)

In this family the flower petals are joined and the flower is often bell-shaped or trumpet-shaped. Each genus has a different shaped style which is typical for that genus. The fruit is a capsule. Many of the species are vines.

Style and stigmas from some Convolvulaceae

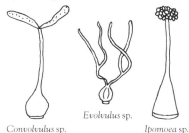

Convolvulus sp.

Evolvulus sp.

Ipomoea sp.

Genus *Convolvulus*

Convolvulus erubescens (Australian bindweed)

Australian bindweed is a perennial vine which is widespread in Australia. It is a very variable species. In CA-NT it can be seen clambering over small plants and larger bushes. The variable leaves are mostly lobed. The pink or white flowers are 10-18 mm wide.

C. *remotus*

This is similar to Australian bindweed, but the leaves are narrower and not lobed, and the hairs are flattened.

Genus *Evolvulus*

Evolvulus alsinoides (Tropical speedwell)

Tropical speedwell is widespread in the tropics. It is a small grey-blue perennial with long silky hairs. The plant grows first erect and then spreads across the ground. The leaves are narrow and pointed. The flowers are blue or white, bell-shaped and 7-8 mm in diameter. There is much variation in this species, with 2 variants in CA-NT.

Convolvulus (Australian bindweed)

Evolvulus alsinoides (Tropical speedwell)

Genus *Ipomoea*

There are 7 *Ipomoea* species found in CA-NT.

Ipomoea polymorpha (Silky cowvine)

This small non-twining annual has a covering of long soft white hairs. The leaves are variable. The pink-purple flower is shaped like a small trumpet 12-16 mm long. Silky cowvine grows in sandy areas. The roots are tuberous and were eaten by the Aborigines.

Ipomoea polymorpha (Silky cowvine)

I. muelleri (Native morning glory)

This is a prostrate perennial with spreading twining stems. The lilac or pink flowers are like trumpets. They are 2.5-4 cm long. The tuberous roots were eaten by the Aborigines.

Ipomoea muelleri (Native morning glory)

I. costata (Rock morning glory, Potato vine, Cow vine)

This vine has large, leathery, dark-green leaves, which are hairless and have prominent veins. The large trumpet-shaped flower is purple-pink, and 7-8 cm long. The vine has large tubers on its roots and these were baked and eaten by the Aborigines.

Ipomoea costata (Rock morning glory, Potato vine, Cow vine)

Boraginaceae (heliotrope family)

In CA-NT, this family includes heliotropes, halganias and cattlebush. *Echium plantagineum* (Patterson's curse), is an introduced member of the family. Boraginaceae are plants which usually have bristly hairs and long narrow flower heads which are rolled up. The fruit usually splits into 4 fruitlets which may be wrinkled, spiny or smooth.

Genus *Heliotropium*

Heliotropium europeum

This is an introduced weed which is poisonous to stock. Some other species are suspected of being poisonous, but most appear not to be eaten by stock.

H. asperrimum (Rough heliotrope)

This small bristly plant has stiff sticky hairs. The small white flowers are in rolled-up spikes. The petals are just seen above the calyx. The fruitlets are wrinkled.

H. curassavicum (Smooth heliotrope)

This is a blue-green, succulent, hairless plant, which is found in damp salty areas. The small white flowers, which are just longer than the 2 mm calyx, are closely packed in 2 rows on a coiled stem. The plant tissue darkens to black as it is dried. Smooth heliotrope is not known to be poisonous.

H. epacrideum

This is a small plant with bristly hairs. The small white flowers are up to 4 mm long and are in rolled-up spikes.

Heliotropium curassavicum (Smooth heliotrope)

Heliotropium epacrideum

Genus *Halgania*

There are several halganias found in CA-NT, and all are very similar. They are small shrubs, up to 50 cm high, with leaves which usually have stiff hairs and are often sticky. The leaves are often narrow and wedge-shaped with a toothed end. The flowers are deep-blue or purple, and are in clusters on long stalks. The flower has a central beak-like projection formed by the stamens surrounding the style. Each anther ends in a long bristle.

Halganias can mainly be distinguished by whether they are sticky (glandular), whether the leaves have hairs, and what kind of hairs these are. (The hairs can be studied with a hand-lens.)

Halgania cyanea

H. cyanea grows 25-30 cm high. Its surface is sticky due to glandular hairs which are stiff and flattened. The leaves are 5-20 mm long. The flower cluster is dense (numerous flowers held closely together).

Halgania cyanea

H. solanacea

The stems and leaves of *H. solanacea* are very glandular, and covered with long soft hairs. The leaves are 2-5 cm long. The flowers are in a loose cluster.

H. erecta

In *H. erecta* the stems and leaves are not sticky. The leaves are covered with stiff flattened hairs and are only 3-10 mm long. There are 1-3 flowers in the cluster.

Halgania erecta

H. glabra

H. glabra is a very sticky plant which has stems and leaves without hairs. The name *glabra* means *hairless*. The leaves are 2-7 cm long. The flowers are in a loose cluster.

Genus *Trichodesma*

Trichodesma zeylanicum (Cattlebush)

Cattlebush can be an annual or perennial. It grows 40 cm-1 m tall, and is usually covered by long stiff hairs, but the hairiness is variable. The clustered flowers are pale-blue, about 2 cm wide and droop downwards. The flower has a central beak-like projection where the stamens surround the style. The anthers end in long bristles which twist together. Cattlebush is seldom grazed.

Trichodesma zeylanicum (Cattlebush)

Verbenaceae (verbena family)

There are 8 genera of this family found naturally in CA-NT. These include *Clerodendrum, Dicrastylis* and *Newcastelia*. Common verbena (*Verbena officinalis*) is an introduced plant originally from the Mediterranean.

Genus *Clerodendrum*

There are several species found in tropical and sub-tropical Australia. They are large bushes with cylindrical branches. The flowers are quite large, and each has a long tube with flared lobes. They are in clusters. After flowering the calyx becomes bright red or purple, and enlarges to hold the fruit which is a juicy black berry.

Clerodendrum floribundum (Smooth spiderbush)

This is called 'yala' by the Aborigines, who still obtain a tuber from the roots. The leaves are wide, dark-green and hairless. The flowers are creamy-white with tubes about 2.5 cm long, and projecting stamens. The calyx is bright-red and the fruit shiny black.

Clerodendrum floribundum (Smooth spiderbush)

Genus *Dicrastylis*

These are small densely hairy shrubs with cylindrical stems, and leaves usually in pairs. The hairs are star-shaped, as can be seen with a hand-lens. The unstalked flowers are in clusters or spikes. The calyx is densely hairy with the flowers almost hidden in the hairs. The name *dicrastylis* comes from Greek and means *forked style*. All *Dicrastylis* species have a forked style. In CA-NT there are 7 different species and several of these have a number of variants. *Dicrastylis* is common on sand-plains and dunes. The species can be distinguished by the disposition of leaves and flowers.

Species with stalked leaves and flowers in branched clusters

Dicrastylis exsuccosa

The flower cluster of this species looks golden-yellow because of yellow hairs.

D. gilesii

This species has hairs which are white or purple.

D. petermannensis

This species is found only in the Petermann Ranges, and has clusters which look grey-green or creamy-yellow.

Dicrastylis exsuccosa

Dicrastylis beveridgei

Species with unstalked leaves and flowers in spikes

D. beveridgei

This species has yellow-woolly flower clusters.

D. costelloi

This species has white-woolly clusters.

D. lewellinii (Purple sand sage)

This species has leaves in clusters, and is covered with grey-woolly hairs. The light blue flowers are in globular clusters.

D. doranii

This is a grey hairy shrub with grey-woolly flower clusters. The flower-spikes are pyramidal in shape. The paired leaves are 1.5-3.5 cm long.

Genus *Newcastelia*

Newcastelia species are found only in Australia and mostly in very dry places. They are small shrubs with a dense covering of star-shaped hairs. The flowers are unstalked and mostly crowded into spikes or heads. The stamens may be inside the flower or projecting. The style is not forked. There are 5 species in CA-NT and these can be distinguished by their fruits.

Newcastelia spodiotricha

This shrub is usually 0.5-1 m high. The densely hairy leaves are paired. They are elliptic, with the edges rolled under and the leaf veins showing clearly beneath. The purple or blue flowers are in oblong spikes with style and stamens projecting. The hairy fruit is inside the calyx.

Newcastelia spodiotricha

Newcastelia spodiotricha

Newcastelia cephalantha

Lamiaceae (mint family)

This family includes sage, mint, rosemary and lavender, and many other plants that have a long history of usefulness to man. The leaves are often strongly scented. The flower is a tube with 2 lips. The fruit has 4 small nuts. There are several genera found in CA-NT.

Genus *Prostanthera*

Prostanthera striatiflora (Striped mintbush)

The name *striatiflora* means *striped flowers*. Striped mintbush grows 1-2 m high, and is very strongly mint-scented. The surface has few or no hairs and the narrow leathery leaves are about 2 cm long. The white flower is bell-shaped with a 2 lobed upper lip and a 3 lobed lower lip with the central lobe largest.

Prostanthera striatiflora (Striped mintbush)

There are purple stripes inside the flower, and yellow spots in the throat. Striped mintbush is found in rocky gorges and near outcrops.

P. wilkeana and *P. baxteri* are also found in CA-NT.

Genus *Plectranthus*

Plectranthus intraterraneus (Purple mintbush)

Purple mintbush is a shrub with soft fleshy leaves and long spikes of purple flowers. The tubular flowers have a bend in the flower-tube and a 4 lobed upper lip with a long lower lip. It is found in creekbeds and rocky gorges, and smells strongly of mint.

Plectranthus intraterraneus (Purple mintbush)

Solanaceae (tomato family)

This family includes our vegetables: potato, tomato, capsicum and egg-plant, as well as tobacco and pituri.

Genus *Solanum* (tomatoes)

In CA-NT these are usually small shrubs 30 cm-1 m high, with a dense hairy covering usually of star-shaped hairs. The detail of the hairs can be seen with a hand-lens. The frilled flowers are mostly in clusters. They are often purple and have the yellow anthers projecting from the centre of each flower, like a beak. The fruits look like small tomatoes, 0.5-3 cm in diameter. They vary in colour and may be green, yellow, brown, red or black. Most are fleshy. Some were eaten by the Aborigines. *Solanum esuriale, S. centrale, S. ellipticum* and *S. cleistogamun* are edible. *S. coactiliferum* is edible after removal of the skin. It is wise only to eat wild tomatoes on advice from a local Aborigine, as some of them are quite poisonous. *S. sturtianum* is poisonous to both humans and stock. It can usually be recognised by the yellow or black dry brittle fruits.

At least 36 species are found in CA-NT. Some of these are described here.

Solanum nigrum (Black berry nightshade)

This species is an introduced weed which has soft simple hairs. The flowers are white and the fruit is a small juicy black berry. It has been considered poisonous, but there is no proof of this. The ripe fruits are edible but the green fruits can be toxic.

Solanum nigrum (Black berry nightshade)

S. quadriloculatum (Wild tomato)

This species has prickles and a dense hairy covering of star-shaped hairs. The leaves are ovate but variable, 6 x 4 cm in size. The flowers are in clusters of 1-10. The fruits are yellow when ripe, and 1-1.5 cm in diameter. This plant can be poisonous to stock, especially the green fruits.

S. orbiculatum (Wild tomato)

This species has a dense hairy covering and prickles which are only on the stem. The leaves are circular to ovate, 3-6 x 3 cm. The flowers are in clusters of 1-4. The yellow fruit is 1.5 cm in diameter.

Solanum orbiculatum (Wild tomato)

Solanum quadriloculatum (Wild tomato)

S. centrale (Desert raisin)

Desert raisin has a rusty-coloured hairy covering, and usually no prickles. The yellow fruit dries brown like a raisin and is edible.

S. esuriale (Quena, Tomato bush)

Quena has a grey or silvery hairy covering, and no prickles. The young leaves are lobed but the adult leaves (3-7 x 1 cm), are not. The pale yellow fruit is edible. It has been suspected of sheep poisoning in NSW, but is not usually grazed.

S. tumicola (Wild tomato)

S. tumicola has no prickles. Its leaves are narrower than Quena (4 cm x 8 mm).

Solanum centrale (Desert raisin)

S. coactiliferum (Western nightshade)

Western nightshade is a grey or silvery plant which usually has prickles on the stems. The leaves are narrow-oblong and slightly recurved. The flowers have 4 petals instead of 5. The yellow fruits are in groups of 1-3. These fruits were roasted by the Aborigines before eating.

S. cleistogamun (Shy nightshade)

Shy nightshade is a low sprawling shrub with prickles. The flowers are slow to open. The fruit is green with a purple flush, and is edible.

Solanum coactiliferum (Western nightshade)

S. ellipticum (Potato bush)

Potato bush is called 'wanki' by the Aborigines. The sprawling bush is pale-green, due to the hairy covering. The prickles are plentiful but may be variable. This plant is very variable. The fruit is about 2 cm in diameter, pale yellow-green, and was eaten by the Aborigines.

S. sturtianum (Thargomindah nightshade, Sturt's nightshade)

Sturt's nightshade can grow up to 2 m high. There is a dense covering of white star-shaped hairs. The leaves are narrow and sometimes wavy (3-6 x 1 cm). The yellow fruit which is dry and brittle, turns black, and it is poisonous. The whole plant is poisonous to stock.

Solanum ellipticum (Potato bush)

Solanum sturtianum (Thargomindah nightshade, Sturt's nightshade)

S. *ferocissimum* (Spiny potato bush)

Spiny potato bush is a very prickly shrub 1-2 m high. It has narrow leaves about 5 cm x 4 mm. The fleshy fruit is 5-8 mm in diameter, and red turning black.

Solanum ferocissimum (Spiny potato bush)

S. *chenopodinum* (Wild tomato)

S. chenopodinum has red fruits, but is less prickly than spiny potato bush, and has lobed leaves.

S. *gilesii* (Wild tomato)

S. gilesii has a covering of rusty-coloured hairs and lobed leaves smaller than 3 x 2 cm.

S. *dioicum* (Wild tomato)

S. dioicum has a covering of rusty-coloured hairs and a large fruit, 2-3 cm in diameter, which is always solitary.

S. *lasiophyllum* (Wild tomato)

S. lasiophyllum has greyish hairs, and leaves that are larger than 3 x 2 cm, and usually not lobed. The fruits (2 cm in diameter) are in a cluster.

S. *petrophilum* (Wild tomato)

S. petrophilum is a low plant found in rocky areas. It has large deep-purple flowers, lobed leaves, and many long prickles.

Genus *Datura* (thornapples)

There are 3 thornapples found in CA-NT: 1 native and 2 introduced. They are low shrubs found mainly along watercourses. The flowers are white and trumpet-shaped, and the leaves wide and coarsely toothed. The seeds are in spiky capsules by which the species can be distinguished. All thornapples are poisonous to stock as well as to people, but are not usually grazed.

Datura leichhardtii (Native thornapple)

This is the local species which is native to CA-NT. The white trumpet-shaped flowers are 4.5-7 cm long. The fruit is round, about 2.5 cm in diameter, and covered with spines up to 9 mm long.

Genus *Nicotiana* (tobaccos)

Nicotiana is the genus from which commercial tobacco is obtained. The Aborigines chew the leaves of the *Nicotiana* species as a narcotic. They usually mixed the leaf material with ash from certain species of acacia and cassia. The species most commonly used for chewing seems to have been *Nicotiana excelsior, N. gossei,* and *N. ingulba.*

There are about 9 species of native tobacco found in CA-NT. All look very similar. They have erect stems, large pointed leaves and terminal clusters of white flowers. The flowers have long narrow tubes, and flaring petals which are shut during the day and open at night. The flowers have a strong scent at night, probably to attract the moths which fertilise them. Some species are hairless. Others are finely haired, often with some glandular hairs. There is one introduced species found in CA-NT, *N. glauca* (Tobacco bush). This is found only near Finke. It is a straggly hairless shrub which can grow into a small tree.

Datura leichhardtii (Native thornapple)

The stems are often bluish. The tube-like flowers are yellow. Tobacco bush comes from Argentina. It is poisonous to both humans and stock, and stock usually avoid it.

Nicotiana excelsior (Native tobacco)

This species has no hairy covering. The leaves are mostly on the stem. The flowers are large: up to 7 cm long with a tube 4 mm wide, and up to 3.5 cm wide at the petal lobes.

172

N. rosulata ssp. ingulba (Native tobacco)

This species is hairless. The leaves are large and mostly basal, and have winged stalks. The flowers are large, 3-5.6 cm long, and up to 2.5 cm wide at the petal lobes.

Nicotiana velutina (Velvet tobacco)

Nicotiana rosulata ssp. ingulba (Native tobacco)

N. velutina (Velvet tobacco)

Velvet tobacco is light blue-green due to a white velvety hairy covering, which is sticky. Most leaves are at the base of the plant. The small stem leaves have winged stalks. The flower is shorter and wider than most, 13-27 mm long with a tube 3.5 mm wide.

N. gossei (Native tobacco)

N. gossei has a dense covering of glandular hairs. The leaves are mostly on the stem, which they clasp. The flower is up to 6.5 cm long.

Nicotiana gossei (Native tobacco)

173

Genus *Duboisia*

Duboisias are shrubs with corky bark, narrow pointed leaves, and bell-shaped white flowers with purple markings inside. The fruits are juicy black berries. Duboisias are important because of the potent alkaloids they contain. In Queensland there are plantations of *Duboisia* hybrids. The leaf is exported for the extraction of hyoscine. The species used are *Duboisia myoporoides* and *D. leichhardtii,* both of which are native to coastal Queensland.

Duboisia hopwoodii (Pituri)

This species is found growing in CA-NT, in south-west Queensland and also in areas of WA. It is widely known because of its use by the Aborigines as a narcotic. The drugs involved are nicotine and nor-nicotine. The drug is obtained by mixing the dried leaves with the ash of certain plants: species of acacia, cassia and supplejack. The mixed wad is then chewed and the alkaline ash helps in the release of the narcotic. The drug 'pituri', which was used in CA-NT, was not obtained from local trees, but by trading from western Queensland. The species *D. hopwoodii* which grows in CA-NT has a higher percentage of nor-nicotine, which is the stronger alkaloid. This makes it too toxic for chewing, but it was used to stupify emus by poisoning waterholes. (The plant is also called Emu poison bush.) The alkaloids make the leaves poisonous to stock. It was calculated that there was enough nor-nicotine in some trees, for just a small amount of leaf to kill a bullock.

Duboisia hopwoodii (Pituri)

Native well, with branch

Scrophulariaceae

This family is found throughout the world. One family member is snapdragon. The characteristically shaped flower has 2 lips and flared lobes. There are many species in CA-NT. They are mainly distinguished by the shape and colour of the flower.

Genus *Stemodia*

Stemodia viscosa

The name *viscosa* means *sticky*. This small, sticky, sprawling shrub is found in moist rocky areas. The plant has a dense covering of glandular hairs, and is strongly mint-scented. The narrow toothed leaves are opposite or whorled. The purple flowers are 5-9 mm long. The petals are striped, with a yellow patch on the lower lip. This plant is widespread in the warmer regions of Australia, and in India, and shows variations in flower and leaf.

has several erect stems with closely clustered narrow leaves. The flowers have two lips, are 1 cm long, and blue or lilac with darker streaks. They crowd up the stems between the leaves. This species is poisonous to sheep and horses, but is usually not grazed.

Morgania floribunda (Blue rod)

Stemodia viscosa

Genus *Morgania*

Morgania floribunda (Blue rod)

Blue rod is found in swampy salty areas near claypans and salt lakes. The plant

Morgania floribunda (Blue rod)

175

Bignoniaceae

Genus *Pandorea*

Pandorea doratoxylon (Spearbush)

Spearbush is a twining climbing shrub
which is found in rocky gorges. The
stems form long canes which were used
by the Aborigines for making spears:
they used to straighten them over a fire.
The leaves are divided into narrow
leaflets. The plant is hairless except for
the inside of the flower. The clustered
flowers are large cream bells with two
lips. Inside the throat they have purple-
brown markings and a mass of hairs.

There are 3 species of *Pandorea* found in
Australia, 1 in CA-NT.

Pandorea doratoxylon (Spearbush)

Myoporaceae

This family includes *Eremophila* (desert
fuchsia) and *Myoporum* (boobialla).

Genus *Myoporum* (boobiallas)

If you hold a boobialla leaf up against
the sun you will see thousands of tiny
glands packed closely together. The
name *myoporum* means *close pores,* and
refers to these glands. The glands help
protect the leaf from heat and insects.
There are a number of boobiallas in
Australia. Boobialla is the Aboriginal
name for one of them. There is only 1
species found in CA-NT.

Myoporum acuminatum (Desert
boobialla, Native myrtle, Western
boobialla)

In the bush, a strong scent of honey may
lead one to where the boobialla grows.
This shrub is 1-2 m high, and has shiny
bright-green leaves which tend to point
up and out. The name *acuminatum*
means *sharp-pointed.* The white bell
flowers stand up on short stems. Inside

Myoporum acuminatum (Desert boobialla,
Native myrtle, Western boobialla)

the flower are purple spots and a white hairy beard. Fruiting is prolific, and the green fruits ripen to purple. Birds love the fruit, especially mistletoe birds. Some boobiallas are poisonous, but the fruit of this boobialla can be eaten by humans and it was an Aboriginal food. Desert boobialla is very drought resistant, and seedlings grow well after rain. It is a good garden plant, but is usually grown from cuttings as the seed capsule is a very hard nut. In Alice Springs it is found in many parks and gardens, especially Undoolya Park. In the bush it is widespread. Visitors to Rainbow Valley will readily find it.

Genus *Eremophila* (desert fuchsias)

Eremophilas are not related to the garden fuchsia plant, but they are commonly called Desert fuchsias. They have many common names: poverty bush, emu bush, turkey bush etc. They are native to Australia, and are found in the dry inland. The name *Eremophila* means *desert lover.* There are 180 species, 27 in CA-NT and many in WA.

Most Desert fuchsias are bushes 1-2 m high, but some are smaller and others larger. Bushes in flower are covered profusely with coloured bells. Flowering depends on the rain. Some species flower 4 or 5 times some years and not at all other years. As is the general rule, plants of each species all flower at the same time. Many species have densely hairy stems and foliage, some are sticky as well as hairy, and some are very sticky and hairless. Leaf shape also varies. Flowers are bell-shaped with lobed or lipped ends. The bell is hairy inside and usually has a covering of soft downy hairs. The style and stamens are either fully inside the flower-tube or else protrude. The flower of each species is constant in shape and characteristics. The calyx is different in each species.

The fruits all have a very hard seed case which may have a fleshy covering, or be dry or very hairy. The fleshy fruits are eaten by bush turkeys and emus, but all are poisonous to humans. Because of the very hard seed case, Desert fuchsias are difficult to grow from seed and most gardeners have only succeeded with cuttings. In the wild, the plants cope well with drought: they drop their leaves during long dry spells, have well-protected seeds which can lie dormant for many years, and show good growth of seedlings after fire and rain. Several Desert fuchsias also multiply by suckering. Desert fuchsias can be seen in many public gardens in Alice Springs, and also at the Olive Pink Flora Reserve.

The Desert fuchsia flower

The bell-shaped flower varies from 1-3 cm long. It has a knob at the base and a tube which ends in lobes or lips of various shapes. There are 7 shapes to consider here. They will be called type A, B, C, D, E, F and G.

Type A flowers

In type A, the flower tube is bell-shaped and ends in 5 forward pointing lobes. The stamens are inside the tube. Desert fuchsias with this shape are *Eremophila christophori* and *E. dalyana.*

Eremophila christophori

Christophori fuchsias make a great display when in bloom. A group of bushes can be seen on the track into John Hayes Rockhole. They are also found near Alice Springs, in the Common south of the town. The tall flowering stems grow straight up, and their stems are covered by small broad green leaves. The flowers crowd closely up each stem amongst the leaves. The flowers are blue but there is a pink variant. The bells end in 5 rounded pointed lobes which turn forward and out. The narrow ovoid fruit is dry, about 5 x 2 mm. The species name *christophori* is a mis-spelling of *christopheri*.

E. dalyana

This is found to the north. The flowers are lilac or white.

Eremophila christophori
Flower – type A

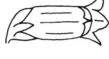

A tube with
5 petals
pointing forwards

Eremophila cristophori

Type B flowers

In type B, the flower tube is bell-shaped with 5 lobes. The 2 upper lobes curve back. The central lower lobe is longer and broader than the others and is notched. The stamens are inside the bell. Fuchsias with this shape are *E. sturtii* and *E. paisleyi*.

E. sturtii (Turpentine bush, Sturt's desert fuchsia)

Turpentine bush is a drooping small bush which is scented and very sticky. The small flowers are white and may have a pink blush, and pink throat spots. The sepals are cream. After flowering the cream petal-like sepals stay on the bush. The small bell-shaped flower is 5 lobed with the larger bottom lobe notched. There is much soft hair both inside and outside the flower. The stems and leaves are sticky but not hairy.

The leaves are narrow and hooked. When crushed the leaves give off a scent of turpentine. The small dry fruit has long soft hairs.

Turpentine bush is not eaten by cattle. Pioneers used the sticky scented leaves as thatch for their meat-houses, to keep the flies away. Turpentine bush is a good drought survivor. It grows well from suckers, and seed germinates after good rains.

Eremophila sturtii
Flower – type B

Eremophila sturtii (Turpentine bush, Sturt's desert fuchsia)

E. paisleyi

This species is a sticky plant which has white or lilac flowers. It differs from *E. sturtii* in that it has stems which are warty (knobbly), longer broader leaves, and smaller sepals. The fruit is small and hairy.

Type C flowers

The type C flower has a longer tube with large lobes which flare out and back forming 2 lips. The upper lip is notched and the lower lip has 3 spreading lobes with the middle lobe larger. There are 6 Desert fuchsias in CA-NT with type C flowers: *E. freelingii, E. gilesii, E. gibsonii, E. goodwinii, E. macdonnellii, E. willsii.*

Eremophila freelingii
Flower – type C

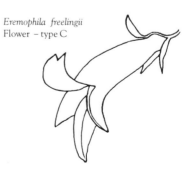

E. freelingii (Rock fuchsia bush)

Rock fuchsia bush is widespread in dry rocky places. These bushes can be seen high up on the walls of the Finke River

179

Gorge and in the amphitheatre at Palm Valley. The tubular flowers have flaring lobes. The sepals turn first brown then purple. The flower is usually lilac but can be pink, blue or white. The fruit is glandular-hairy. Rock fuchsia is a real survivor.The bushes can look more dead than alive, with dry greyish leaves in a drooping bunch sheltering a drooping flower. The usually soft hairy leaves become streaked with resin and many drop from the stem. When there is a little rain the plant revives. After good rains the plant is transformed: tissues become lush, stems and leaves point outwards and even the flowers look rounder and less fragile. This species is considered poisonous to stock, but in CA-NT it is not usually in accessible places.

E. gilesii (Desert fuchsia, Giles' desert fuchsia)

This species was named after the explorer Giles, who first collected it. The bush is usually no more than 1 m high, and is readily recognised by the profusion of scattered blue or lilac bell-shaped flowers. The leaves are long and narrow, and hooked, but are variable and may be toothed. The plant has a hairy and sticky covering, but the hairs vary from dense to sparse. Hairy leaves are greyer and the less hairy are green. The flower is on a long S-shaped stalk. The flower shape is type C, and has fine white down outside and a thick white beard inside. The fruit is a distinctive small hairy ball which hangs down on its stalk. Giles' desert fuchsia does not tolerate fire well.

E. gibsonii (Gibson's desert fuchsia)

Gibson's fuchsia is found in the sand dune country. It can be readily seen on the dunes as it is a large bright-green bush growing to 2 m high. The bush is very sticky and not hairy. The narrow sticky bright-green leaves are hooked

Eremophila freelingii (Rock fuchsia bush)

Eremophila gilesii (Desert fuchsia, Giles' desert fuchsia)

and may have toothed edges. The type C flower has a very rounded tube and short lobes, with fine downy hair outside the tube. It may be pink, blue or white. The narrow ovoid fruit is 4.5-6 mm long, ribbed and sticky.

Eremophila gibsonii (Gibson's desert fuchsia)

Eremophila gibsonii (Gibson's desert fuchsia)

E. macdonnellii (Macdonnell's desert fuchsia)

This plant was named after Sir Richard Macdonnell, who was governor of SA at the time. Macdonnell fuchsia is low and spreading, and flowers when 30-50 cm high. The flower is deep purple with the tube flaring into an upper notched lip and 3 spreading lower lobes. The short leaves have no stalks and vary from narrow to broad. The plant has a hairy covering which varies from dense to sparse. There are several varieties. The large juicy fruit is globular, and up to 1.5 cm in diameter. Macdonnell's fuchsia could be confused with Wills' fuchsia which is also deep purple. Wills' fuchsia always has a darker throat spot, and a white beard inside the upper lip.

Eremophila macdonnellii (Macdonnell's desert fuchsia)

E. goodwinii (Purple fuchsia bush)

Purple fuchsia bush is a small, hairy, sticky shrub often found in rocky areas. The lilac flower has a notched upper lip and 3 flaring lower lobes. It is an erect plant with the flower held up on a stiff

Eremophila goodwinii (Purple fuchsia bush)

hairy stem, and narrow deep-green leaves which have no stalks. Both sepals and flower stalk have both short and long hairs. The hairy conical fruit is held erect.

E. willsii (Sandhill native fuchsia, Wills' desert fuchsia)

Sandhill fuchsia will always be found growing in deep sand, especially in dune areas. It is seen frequently in the dune country of south-west CA-NT. It is a good desert survivor and reproduces from suckers and from seedlings which often germinate after fire. Sandhill fuchsia is not large. The bush grows as several erect stems to about 1 m.

The plant has a glandular hairy surface. The short green leaves have no stalks. They vary in shape, but are often triangular with serrated edges. The large flowers are usually bright-purple, but may be lilac. They always have a very dark throat spot and a fringed white beard under the upper lip. The fruit is egg-shaped.

In CA-NT the following are other Desert fuchsias with type C flowers:

E. cordatisepala
Flower light-blue; fruit: shiny, ribbed and beaked.

Eremophila willsii (Sandhill native fuchsia, Wills' desert fuchsia)

E. elderi
Flower light-blue; fruit: large and pear-shaped.

E. exotrachys
Fruit: hairy and egg-shaped.

E. hughesii
Flower light-blue; fruit: hairy, ribbed and beaked.

E. obovata
Flower blue with rounded lobes.

E. ovata
Flower lilac; fruit: densely hairy.

E. rotundifolia
Flower blue, the egg-shaped fruit hairy.

Type D flowers

The flower tube is broad and bell-shaped with 5 broad lobes. The lowest lobe is larger and longer, and divided. Desert fuchsias with type D flowers are *E. bignoniiflora* and *E. polyclada.*

E. bignoniiflora (Gooramurra)

Gooramurra occurs to the north of Alice Springs. It is tall (up to 4 m), and hairless, and has long leaves. The flowers are cream, tinged with red. There are purple spots inside and on the lower lobe. The stamens are visible inside. The egg-shaped fleshy fruit is eaten by emus. Aborigines used the fruit as a purgative and the leaves as a laxative. The plant is good as sheep fodder. It has been suspected of toxicity but there is no proof of this.

E. polyclada (Flowering lignum)

This plant looks like lignum, and like lignum, is found growing near claypans. The bell-shaped flower is white, with green or brown spots, and has a deep indentation of the lower lobe. The oblong pointed fruit is 1-1.5 cm long.

Eremophila ovata

Eremophila flower – type D
E. bignoniiflora

(A true lignum has much smaller flowers and fruit, striated branches, and leaves which drop very early.)

184

Type E flowers

Type E flowers have a curved bell-shaped
tube with an open mouth, and the
stamens project under the 2 upper lobes.
The 3 bottom lobes curve right back.
The knob at the base of the flower is
very prominent. Species with type E
flowers are *E. latrobei*, *E. longifolia*, and
E. neglecta.

E. latrobei (Native fuchsia, Latrobe's desert fuchsia)

Latrobe's fuchsia is easily recognised
when in flower, as the bush is covered
with bright-red flower bells. The bells
curve downwards with wide mouth and
extended stamens. The leaves vary from
narrow, green and almost hairless, to
wider, hairy and grey-green. The sepals
also vary from green to brown, with the
hairs dense or sparse. The conical fruit
is not hairy. This fuchsia is widespread
in arid Australia, and is both drought
tolerant and fire resistant. In CA-NT
it is widespread. It is freely grazed and
recovers well. Flowering occurs in
response to rainfall.

E. longifolia (Weeping emu bush, Long-leafed desert fuchsia)

Weeping emu bush is a generally
accepted common name. The name
longiflora means *long-leafed*. Weeping
emu bush is a drooping bush or small
tree which may be difficult to distin-
guish from the many other small
drooping trees of the dry inland. The
special features of leaf and flower will
need to be looked for. The drooping
dull-green leaves are narrow, and up to
15 cm long. They are usually only
sparsely haired. The flowers are often
hidden amongst the foliage, but during
dry periods when many leaves drop, the
flowers and fruits may be seen on stalks
emerging from the branches. The flower
shape is type E, with rounded lobes and
a very prominent knob. The curving

Eremophila latrobei (Native fuchsia,
Latrobe's desert fuchsia)

Eremophila flower – type E
E. latrobei

flower tube is brick-red with spotting inside and fine hairs on the outside. The fleshy fruit becomes purple when ripe, and is eaten by both cattle and emus.

This Desert fuchsia is widespread in CA-NT and all the dry inland. Because of a tendency to suckering, the bushes often grow in groves. It is good cattle fodder and recovers well, and is the most important Desert fuchsia used for topfeed. It recovers well after fire.

E. neglecta

The word *neglecta* means *overlooked*. This is a sticky shrub with hairless leaves. The flowers are red or brown, and the sepals purple. The flower shape is type E with rounded lobes. The wrinkled fruit has 2 angles and is beaked.

Eremophila longifolia (Weeping emu bush, Long-leafed desert fuchsia)

Type F flowers

The type F flower is bell-shaped with a gaping mouth. The upper lip has 4 lobes. The lower lip cuts the tube deeply and curves right back. The stamens protrude. Desert fuchsias with type F flowers are *E. maculata*, *E. glabra*, *E. duttonii*, *E. serrulata* and *E. alternifolia*.

E. maculata (Spotted fuchsia)

The name *maculata* means *spotted*. Spotted fuchsia grows to about 1.5 m. The branches and leaf stalks are softly hairy, but the dark-green leaves are hairless or sparsely haired. The leaves point up and outwards. The flowers are on long S-shaped stalks. The globular fleshy fruit becomes dry. It is large, 1.5-2 cm in diameter. Many of the Desert fuchsia species have spotted flowers, but only *E. maculata* (Spotted fuchsia) always has them. There are 2 local varieties; one with narrow leaves and the other with oval leaves .

Eremophila flower – type F
E. maculata (Spotted fuchsia)

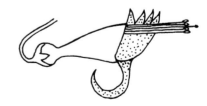

Spotted fuchsia has been found to be toxic to stock at certain times in some places. The new young leaves are the most poisonous. The problem seems worse when animals are tired or hungry. However, in many places it is grazed heavily without problems.

Eremophila maculuta (Spotted fuchsia)

Eremophila glabra (Black fuchsia)

E. glabra (Black fuchsia)

This is a very variable plant which is very sticky. It may be prostrate or erect and the leaves and stems vary from almost hairless to very hairy. Leaf colour varies from bright-green to dark-green. The name *glabra* means *hairless*. The flowers are yellow, orange or red, with a very short stalk of 2 mm.

E. duttonii (Harlequin fuchsia bush)

This species grows as a bush 1-3 m high and has crowded shiny dark-green leaves which are often dropped. The type F flower is on a long S-shaped stalk. The flowers are red above, and yellow below and inside. The sepals are long and wide. The pear-shaped fruit is up to 1 cm long.

E. serrulata (Green fuchsia bush, Toothed fuchsia bush)

This small very sticky shrub has shiny bright-green toothed leaves. The green flowers are on long S-shaped stalks. The flower tube is covered with small sticky hairs. The small round fruit is hairless.

E. alternifolia (Scented emu bush, Narrow-leafed fuchsia bush)

This fuchsia bush has a strong scent like honeysuckle. It grows 1-2 m tall, and is hairless. The branches are warty (knobbly) and the young growth is sticky. The leaf is very narrow almost terete, often with a curved end. The flower is deep pink with red spots in the throat. Its shape is type F, with open mouth, 4 upper lobes and a lower lobe curved well back. The stamens are inside the upper lip. The broad papery sepals overlap and may be purple. The flower is on a long S-shaped stalk. The fleshy succulent fruit is about 6 mm long. Scented emu bush is found in the western sand dune area of CA-NT and northern SA, usually near rocky hills. Bushes can be found near Ayers Rock on the eastern side. There could be some difficulty in distinguishing E. alternifolia from E. maculata. In E. alternifolia the stamens do not protrude beyond the upper lip, spotting may not always occur, there is no hairiness at all and the strong scent is very characteristic. Both species have fleshy fruits, but that of Scented emu bush is half the size of Spotted fuchsia fruit.

Type G flowers

This flower is bell-shaped with a wide mouth, notched upper lip, 2 lateral lobes curved back, and a large lower lobe curved back. The stamens protrude.

E. leucophylla (White-leafed desert fuchsia)

This small Desert fuchsia has branches and leaves covered with a dense white hairy coat. The name *leucophylla* means *white leaf*. The flower is pink or yellow-pink and is on a long S-shaped stalk. The fruit is hairless, and about 8 mm long. This Desert fuchsia grows mainly in the western desert areas.

Eremophila flower – type G

Campanulaceae (bluebell family)

There are over 2000 species of Campanulaceae spread throughout the world, in temperate and sub-tropical regions. In CA-NT they include *Wahlenbergia* (bluebells), *Isotoma* (rock isotome) and *Lobelia*.

The leaves are not divided. The bell-shaped flowers have a tube and 3-5 petals. In some genera the flower is split and has 2 lips. The stamens are free, or else fused in a tube around the style. The fruit is a capsule.

Genus *Wahlenbergia* (bluebells)

The bluebell genus includes both annuals and perennials. They have a fleshy taproot and sometimes underground stems. The stems above ground are erect, terete, and sometimes branched. Bluebells may be hairy or almost hairless. The leaves are at the base of the plant and on the lower stems, and the flowers are on long leafless stalks. The leaf margins are toothed and may be flat or wavy. The bell-shaped flower is usually blue and symmetrical, with 5 petals. The stamens are free, and the style has 2, 3 or 5 branches. The seed capsule develops inside the calyx, which does not drop after flowering.

Bluebells are distinguished by the leaves (lower leaves alternate or opposite), the size and shape of the flower petals, and the shape of the seed capsule. There are several species found in CA-NT.

Wahlenbergia communis (Tufted bluebell)

This species is a perennial. It grows in tufts, which are connected by underground stems. The plant is usually hairless, and grows 15-60 cm tall. The leaves are alternate and narrow (1-8 cm x 1-6 mm). The flower is usually blue, and has petals 6-13 mm long. The style has 3 ends. The seed capsule is 4-9 mm long and shaped like a spinning top.

Wahlenbergia (bluebell) – now identified as *W. species C*

W. gracilis (Australian bluebell)

This is a perennial which grows in tufts, with flower stems 10-50 cm tall. The plant is hairless or sparsely haired. The leaves are alternate, sometimes with the lower leaves opposite. They are usually narrow, 2-6 cm x 2-10 mm. The flower is blue with petals 1.5-6 mm long. The style usually has 3 ends. The seed capsule is top-shaped 2.5-7 mm long.

There are 3 other species found in CA-NT. At present these are called *Wahlenbergia Sp. A, Sp. B, and Sp. C.*

Genus *Isotoma*

Isotomes grow as much-branched herbs, which have milky white sap. The leaves are usually toothed. The flower is lilac, white or blue, and is on a long stalk. The flowers have a narrow tube with spreading petals, and often have markings on the lower 3 petals. The stamens form a tube around the style. There is a 2 lobed stigma. The seed-capsule is inside the calyx.

There are about 12 species, mostly Australian, with only one in CA-NT.

Isotoma petraea (Rock isotome)

This is a perennial which is found amongst rocky outcrops and hillsides. It is a prostrate to ascending plant which has much-branched stems up to 40 cm long. The white sap is astringent and may be harmful if it gets into the eyes. The leaves are pale-green, and toothed, up to 7 cm long. The petals are lilac, or white tinged with blue, 9-12 mm long, and pointed. The seed-capsule is cylindrical.

Isotoma petraea (Rock isotome)

Genus *Lobelia*

Lobelias are hairless plants which stand erect. They have alternate leaves and irregular flowers. The flower is purple or white, and is split on one side making 2 lips. The upper lip usually has 2 smaller petals, and the lower lip 3 larger.

Lobelia heterophylla

This is the only lobelia found in CA-NT. It is an erect herb growing to 40 cm. The stem leaves tend to be lobed or toothed, and the basal ones are not. The flower is pale-blue with yellow in the throat, and is 1.5-2 cm long. The capsule is cylindrical to globular.

Lobelia heterophylla – flower

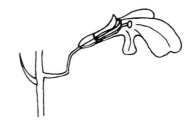

Goodeniaceae (goodenia family)

This family can be recognised by the flower, which has a split tube with 2 lips, and winged petals. The style has a small cup on its end. The seeds are mostly flat and often rimmed by a wing. Most of the species in this family are Australian. In CA-NT the family includes *Goodenia, Scaevola, Dampiera, Lechenaultia, Velleia,* and *Catosperma*.

Genus *Goodenia*

There are 170 *Goodenia* species, mostly Australian, with 21 found in CA-NT. Most have yellow or blue flowers. The flower is split, with 2 upper and 3 lower petals. All the petals have frill-like wings. The seeds are usually in a capsule.

In CA-NT there are over 20 yellow-flowered goodenias and several blue-flowered species. The blue-flowered goodenias are G. *vilmoriniae,* G. *azuria,* G. *ramelii* and a blue variety of G. *grandiflora*.

Goodenia lunata (Hairy goodenia)

This is a small hairy perennial up to 30 cm high. The leaves are mostly at the base, and are 4-7 cm long. They are usually toothed or lobed. The yellow flower is about 15 mm long, and is held erect on a hairy stalk 2-7 cm long. The seed capsule is egg-shaped, about 1 cm long. The flattened seed is ringed by a wing.

Seed capsule of *Goodenia lunata* (Hairy goodenia) is about 5 mm diameter with seed surrounded by wing

Goodenia lunata (Hairy goodenia)

G. *fascicularis*

This is very similar to G. *lunata*. The distinction is in the style-cup.

G. *cycloptera* and G. *heterochila* (Serrated goodenia)

These two yellow flowered goodenias are similar, with erect leafy stems to about 40 cm. The basal leaves are large,

Goodenia cycloptera (Serrated goodenia)

191

toothed, softly hairy, and almost without stalks. The stem leaves are shorter and narrower. The flowers are 10-15 mm long. The seed-capsule is globular and the flattened seeds are winged. The species can be distinguished by the style-cup.

Goodenia heterochila (Serrated goodenia)

Goodenia modesta (goodenia)

G. modesta (Goodenia)

This graceful yellow-flowered goodenia is found in moist low-lying areas. The leaves and stems are dark-green and hairless or sparsely haired. The basal leaves are up to 8 cm long, and may be toothed or lobed. The flowers are 10-15 mm long, on leafy erect stems. The seeds are tiny.

G. gibbosa (Goodenia)

This goodenia spreads by runners which put out roots and shoots at intervals. Each shoot has a rosette of leaves, and the yellow flowers are on long stalks. The flower is about 15 mm long and has a marked nectary pocket. The black seed is flat and round, with a grey wing

Goodenia gibbosa (goodenia)

G. armitiana (Goodenia)

This yellow goodenia is found to the north of Alice Springs. The fine erect stems are hairless. The narrow stem leaves have no stalks, and are 2-6 cm long. They are glandular and may be softly haired. The yellow flowers are 8-10 mm long. The seed capsule is on an erect stalk.

G. virgata (Goodenia)

This species is similar to G. armitiana, but the leaves have no hairs, and the fruiting stalks extend out or downwards.

G. grandiflora (Mountain primrose)

This large-flowered goodenia can be yellow, blue or white. It is an erect shrub up to 80 cm tall. The toothed leaves are wide, pointed, and 2-6 cm long. They have soft simple hairs, and are sticky. The striking flower is 2-2.5 cm long. The elliptic seeds have a narrow wing. The blue flowered variety can be seen at Standley Chasm.

Goodenia grandiflora (Mountain primrose)

Goodenia armitiana (goodenia)

G. vilmoriniae (Goodenia)

This is a small erect silky-haired herb
with a basal rosette of leaves. The
flowers are in clusters on erect stalks.
They are blue to lilac, 1.5-2 cm long,
with fine glandular hairs outside.
The flat round seeds are brown or black,
with a broad wing.

Goodenia vilmoriniae (goodenia)

Genus *Lechenaultia*

This genus was named after a French
botanist, Leschenault, but was
originally recorded without the s.
Lechenaultias are small shrubs, mostly
with narrow leaves. The split flower-
tube has 2 small upper petals and
3 larger lower petals which may be
winged. The style-cup has 2 lips.
Most lechenaultias are found in WA.
There are 3 species in CA-NT.

Lechenaultia divaricata (Tangled lechenaultia)

The word *divaricata* means *forked*.
Tangled lechenaultia is a small round
hairless shrub about 30-60 cm high.
It has much-divided tangled stems
which have no leaves, as the leaves have
been reduced to scales. The flower is
1.5-2 cm long and is white, blue or
yellow. The upper 2 petals are almost
wingless, and the lower 3 petals have
frilled wings. The fruit is a dry
cylindrical capsule bulging over several
enclosed seeds. The Aborigines
obtained a resin from the root.

Lechenaultia divaricata (Tangled lechenaultia)

Genus *Dampiera*

Dampieras are small shrubs usually with blue or lilac flowers. The flower-tube is split so that there are 2 frilled petals above and 3 below. The style has a globular cup. The calyx is usually very densely haired. The fruit is a dry capsule. There are 60-65 species, all native to Australia. There are 3 in CA-NT.

Dampiera cinerea

D. cinerea is often found on sand dunes. It is a much-branched shrub about 50 cm high, and looks silver-grey because of a dense hairy covering. The narrow leaves are mostly near the base and the small stalked flowers are on leafless spikes. They are about 7 mm long, and have a very hairy calyx. The petals are purple-blue, and have long narrow wings.

D. candicans

This also has purple-blue flowers, but the wings on the petals are short. The flower is 7 mm long, and the calyx has a dense covering of brown and white hairs. The leaves are oval and toothed, and hairless on the upper surface.

Dampiera cinerea

Genus *Scaevola* (fanflower)

In *Scaevola* the flower-tube is split so that all the petals are together on one side, forming a fan. The flowers are 1-2 cm long, and may be blue, lilac or white. The name *scaevola* comes from a Latin word meaning *left-handed*, because of the one-sided shape. There are about 90 species, which are mostly Australian, and 7 are found in CA-NT. The specific differences are in the style-cup and the seed capsule. There are general differences in leafiness and hairiness.

Scaevola collaris

S. collaris is a small, scented, hairless shrub which grows near salt-lakes. The leaves are narrow, and thick. The flower is large (up to 2 cm long), and lilac or white. The ribbed cylindrical pod is hairless, 1.5-2 cm long, and ends in a neck-like projection.

S. spinescens (Spiny fanflower)

Spiny fanflower is a rigid, spiny, hairy shrub which is well-grazed by stock. It can grow into a bush up to 2 m high. The leaves are thick and greyish, up to 2 cm long. The fan-shaped flowers are white, with fringed petals. The fruit is a black or purple juicy berry about 8 mm in diameter. It is edible, and was an Aboriginal food.

Scaevola collaris

Scaevola spinescens (Spiny fanflower)

S. *depauperata* (Skeleton fanflower)

Skeleton fanflower is found on sand dunes. It has most of the leaves reduced to scales. The hairless stems are striated (striped lengthwise). The flower is white or lilac, 2-2.5 cm long. The fruit is a warty, oblong capsule.

Scaevola depauperata (Skeleton fanflower)

S. *basedowii*

S. *basedowii* is similar to skeleton fanflower, but the stems are hairy and glandular. It is also found among the sand dunes.

S. *parvifolia*

The name *parvifolia* means *few leaves*, and this plant has few leaves. The stems are covered with coarse spreading hairs, and the flower is blue.

S. *ovalifolia*

S. *ovalifolia* is a densely-hairy small perennial with roundish toothed leaves. The flowers can be blue, white or yellow. There are several variants.

S. *laciniata*

This scaevola is similar to S. *ovalifolia*, but has no hairs. The flowers are blue.

Scaevola ovalifolia
(fanflower)

Scaevola parvifolia (fanflower)

Genus *Velleia*

Velleia connata

This is an erect herb which can grow to 60 cm. It has a strong taproot, large leaves at the base of the plant, and the flowers on branching stems. Below the flower there is a funnel-shaped collar of leafy bracts. The flower is up to 18 mm long, and yellow, yellow-brown, or white. Stock do not graze the plant.

There are 2 other species of *Velleia* found in CA-NT.

Velleia connata

Brunoniaceae (Brunonia family)

Brunonia australis (Blue pincushion)

Blue pincushion looks like a daisy because it has flower-heads made up of many small flowers clustered together. The cornflower-blue heads are on leafless stalks 10-30 cm long, with the leaves crowded at the base of the plant. The tiny flowers are tubular with blue petal-like lobes. Each small flower is enclosed in a hairy tube. The style is not forked like the daisy, but has a cup on the end. The small seeds are nuts. Blue pincushion is found in sandy areas. The family is unusual in that it consists of only this one species.

Brunonia australis (Blue pincushion)

Asteraceae (daisy family)
– also called Compositae

Most of us think of a daisy as a flower, with a yellow centre and one or more rows of petals. However, this is not one flower, but a flower head, in which many tiny flowers are bunched closely together on a flat disc or cone-shaped plate, the receptacle. This disc is formed by a widening of the end of the stem. The disc is sometimes smooth, but in some genera there are either chaffy scales or bristles attached to the surface. The small flowers of a daisy-head can be seen clearly in a sunflower. In the centre can be seen tiny yellow flowers which are tubular with a toothed edge. These are called disc flowers. The outer flowers are also small, but have a tongue-like projection on one side. We usually call this a petal. The technical name is

Daisy – cross-section of flower head (taken from Sunflower)

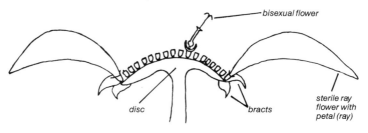

bisexual flower

disc

bracts

sterile ray flower with petal (ray)

Daisy flowers (much enlarged)

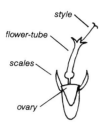

Bisexual disc flower

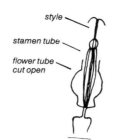

Inside the bisexual flower

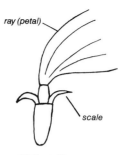

Sterile ray flower

'a ray'. These small flowers are called ray flowers. In daisies, some of the many flowers in a head are bisexual, some male, and some female. In daisy flowers the style has a forked end. The stamens are usually fused together, and to the style. The sepals are modifed into bristles or scales which together form a crown around the top of the seed. This crown is often feathery and is called 'the pappus'. It assists in spreading seeds on the wind, as seen in a dandelion. In daisies with spiky or hooked bristles the seeds may form burrs.

In everlastings, the petals are not formed by flowers, but by the various shaped ends of bracts. Bracts are modified leaves which surround the flower head just like sepals surround an individual flower. The rows of bracts together form an 'involucre', which is the cup-like back of the flower head. This can be fleshy or papery.

Individual species can be identified by the shape of seed and pappus. For the identification of a daisy, the collection of a seed-head is helpful.

Daisies are a very successful family, the largest family of flowering plants in the world, with about 22,000 species. As well as efficient seed dispersal, daisies are successful because the many tiny flowers in a head open one after the other. This allows fertilisation by many pollen grains and so increases the genetic mix. Some daisies are annuals, others perennials. Annuals succeed by rapid growth to flowering and seeding. Perennials succeed by shooting again when conditions are right, by budding from roots, and suckering.

Such a large family has many genera. To simplify classification, botanists group these into tribes. Some of these tribes are: asters, sunflowers, buttons, groundsells (yellowtops), marigolds, everlastings, Scotch thistles and milk thistles.

The name Asteraceae comes from a Greek word *aster* meaning *a star*. The family is also called Compositae because of the composite nature of its flower head. Nowadays all family botanical names are based on the first described genus in the family. In the case of daisies, this is the *Aster* genus.

Minuria and *Brachycome*

Minuria and *Brachycome* species are similar small daisies with soft petals.

The main difference is in the seeds. The flower head has a centre formed from yellow tubular flowers, and several rows of ray flowers which form petals that are usually white, blue, pink or lilac. The flower heads are hemispherical, and surrounded by several rows of bracts. In *Minuria* the leaves alternate up the stem, and are usually not lobed or divided. *Minuria* seeds each have a crown of fine bristles which is usually as long as the seed or longer. Minurias are only found in Australia, with 5 species in CA-NT. *Brachycome* may have its leaves at the base of the plant or up the stem. The leaves are usually toothed or much divided. *Brachycome* seeds each have a tiny crown of hair-like bristles which are shorter than the seed. The name *brachycome* comes from Greek and means *short hairs*. Brachycomes are found mainly in Australia, 3 in CA-NT.

Genus *Minuria*

Minuria leptophylla (Minnie daisy)

Minnie daisy is commonly seen in clumps 10-30 cm high. The flower stems are hairy. The leaves are straight and narrow, 1-2 cm x 1-2 mm. The name *leptophylla* means *narrow leaves*. The genus name *Minuria* probably comes from the Greek word *minyros* meaning *thin* (because of the thin leaves of this *Minuria*). The flower heads are 2-3 cm in diameter, have a yellow centre, and soft white to lilac petals about 1 cm long. Several rows of pointed fringed bracts form a bell-shaped cup for the flower head. The tiny seeds have feathery bristles about the same length as the seed. This daisy is grazed by stock and is a useful fodder.

M. denticulata (Woolly minuria)

Woolly minuria is a hairy perennial which grows to 40 cm. The leaves are 1-3 cm x 2-4 mm, and are toothed towards the tip. The flower heads have a yellow centre and blue petals up to 5 mm

Minuria leptophylla (Minnie daisy) – seed of disc flower is about 2 mm long with bristles of about the same length

Brachycome ciliaris (Variable daisy) – seed of disc flower is about 2.5-3 mm long with very short bristles

long. It is especially found in floodout areas.

M. integerrima (Smooth minuria)

Smooth minuria is a hairless erect plant which grows up to 40 cm high. The leaves are 2-3 cm long, and not toothed. The many petals are blue or lilac, 2-4 mm long, and very narrow. This daisy is widespread, found especially on river banks.

M. cunninghamii (Bush minuria)

Bush minuria is a hairless erect shrubby plant 15-50 cm high. The narrow leaves are 1-2 cm long, hooked, but not toothed. Bush minuria is widespread on sand plains, creekbeds and in salty areas. It is palatable to stock, and a good fodder plant.

Minuria leptophylla (Minnie daisy)

Minuria integerrima (Smooth minuria)

Genus *Brachycome*

There are several brachycomes found in CA-NT. They are very similar but vary in the seed. *B. ciliaris* is the best known.

Brachycome ciliaris (Variable daisy)

Variable daisy is a small perennial which is widespread in mainland Australia. It grows only to 40 cm and is often less than 20 cm high. It usually has a fine glandular hairy covering, but can be hairless or quite woolly. The leaves are up to 4 cm long, and divided into 3-9 narrow pointed lobes which are usually toothed. The flower heads have a yellow centre and white or lilac petals about 5 mm long. The species is called *ciliaris* because of the cilia or fine soft hairs which fringe the bracts. The shape of the seed and its crown distinguishes this daisy from others like it.

Genus *Calotis* (burr daisies)

There are about 20 species of *Calotis*, which is only found in Australia. The name comes from the Greek words *kalos* meaning *beautiful,* and *otos* meaning *ear.* It refers to the 2 ear-like spines of the seeds of one species. The most obvious features of *Calotis* are the seed-heads, which are usually in the form of burrs. The seed has a crown of stiff bristles or spines and the seed of each species can be identified by its shape. *Calotis* includes both annuals and perennials. The leaves mostly alternate up the stem. The flower heads have yellow tubular flowers in the centre, surrounded by petals which are yellow, white, blue or lilac. The heads feel rough because the supporting bracts have rough edges.

Calotis erinacea (Tangled burr daisy)

The name *erinacea* comes from the Greek word for *hedgehog.* Tangled burr daisy is a yellow daisy, with yellow centre and yellow petals. The bush is a perennial, 30-50 cm high, with smooth

Brachycome ciliaris (Variable daisy)

Calotis erinacea (Tangled burr daisy)

tangled stems. The leaves are oblong or wedge-shaped, mostly with toothed edges. The flower heads are about 2 cm wide. The seed has a crown with 2-9 barbed spines, and the seed-heads are burrs. This daisy is found around limestone outcrops and in sandy areas, especially on dunes. It helps to hold the sand together.

C. cymbacantha (Showy burr daisy)

Showy burr daisy has a yellow centre and yellow petals. It is a hairy erect perennial, with oblong, wedge-shaped or pointed leaves which are usually toothed. The name *cymbacantha* means *boat-shaped prickles,* and refers to the shape of the spines on the seed. The seed-heads are burrs.

C. cuneifolia (Purple burr daisy)

Purple burr daisy grows 20-60 cm high, and is covered with stiff hairs. The leaves are wedge-shaped and toothed. The name *cuneifolia* means *wedge leaves.* The flower heads have lilac, blue or white petals, and a yellow centre. The seeds are wedge-shaped with 2-4 barbed spines, and the seed-head is a burr.

Calotis cuneifolia (Purple burr daisy)

Calotis seeds with spines

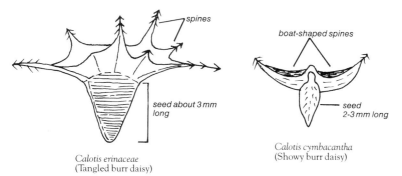

spines

seed about 3 mm long

Calotis erinaceae (Tangled burr daisy)

boat-shaped spines

seed 2-3 mm long

Calotis cymbacantha (Showy burr daisy)

205

C. hispidula (Bogan flea, Bindyeye)

Bogan flea is a widespread small daisy which has a rough and hairy surface. The flower heads are greenish with tiny yellow petals up to 1 mm long. The bracts are very rough to touch. The seed has 5-6 spreading spines, and forms a very prickly burr which is troublesome to stock, especially sheep. The burr can penetrate bare feet and cause much irritation.

C. latiuscula (Leafy burr daisy)

Leafy burr daisy is an erect perennial which has a roughened surface. The flower head has a yellow centre and yellow petals. The toothed leaves are up to 5 cm long, and are mostly on the stem. The flattened wedge-shaped seed has numerous spines at the top.

Calotis hispidula (Bogan flea, Bindyeye)

petals, *C. squamigera* with tiny petals (less than 1 mm long), and *C. porphyroglossa* with purple petals.

Calotis latiuscula (Leafy burr daisy)

C. plumulifera (Woolly-headed burr daisy) – previously C. multicaulis

This species has white or purple petals. It is an annual 6-50 cm high, with a rough hairy surface. The hairy seed has a crown of flexible hairy bristles (12-24) which are up to 2.5 cm long.

Other local *Calotis* species are: *C. kempei* and *C. lappulacea,* both with yellow

Calotis plumulifera – previously *C. multicaulis* (Woolly-headed burr daisy)

Genus *Ixiochlamys*

Ixiochlamys occurs only in Australia. The flower head has a centre of tubular flowers, and many rows of ray flowers forming very narrow petals. The bell-shaped heads are on long leafless stalks. Each seed has a brush of long soft feathery bristles on a fine stalk-like filament.

Ixiochlamys cuneifolia (Silverton daisy)

This delightful small daisy is found on river banks in floodout areas. The flower head is on a stalk up to 25 cm long. There are numerous very narrow white petals. The narrow pointed bracts are hairy and very sticky. The wedge-shaped leaves have a toothed end. They are hairy and sticky, and crowd at the base of the stem. The name *cuneifolia* means *wedge leaves*. The seed heads are feathery.

Ixiochlamys cuneifolia (Silverton daisy)

Ixiochlamys cuneifolia (Silverton daisy) – seed with stalk and feathery brush

Genus *Olearia* (daisy bushes)

Olearia are perennials, and are found only in Australia, Papua New Guinea and New Zealand. The flower heads have both disc and ray flowers. There is only 1 row of ray flowers and not all form petals, so petals tend to be few. The bracts have rough edges. The seeds have a crown of fine bristles.

Olearia subspicata (Spiked daisy bush)

Spiked daisy bush is a perennial, 1-2 m high, with velvety branches. The flower heads are narrow-cylindrical. The name *subspicata* means *almost spiked*. The narrow heads do not contain many flowers, usually 3-4 disc flowers and 1 row of ray flowers forming only 2-3 petals. The petals are white. The leaves are straight and narrow with rolled edges. The seed has a crown of 40-50 bristles.

Olearia subspicata (Spiked daisy bush)

O. stuartii

This is a straggly shrub, 30-60 cm high, with a glandular hairy surface. It can be found at Standley Chasm. The leaves are up to 2 cm long, and are often toothed. The flower heads may be 2-3 cm in diameter, with lilac petals 6-10 mm long.

O. ferresii

This erect sticky shrub grows to 1 m high, and is hairless. The flower heads are large, with white petals up to 14 mm long, and a large yellow centre of tubular flowers. The strongly scented leaves are 4-10 cm long.

Olearia stuartii (daisy bush)

Olearia ferresii (daisy bush)

Genus *Helianthus* (sunflowers)

Helianthus annua (Sunflower)

Sunflower is an introduced daisy which is native to North America. It is cultivated world-wide as a garden flower, and for its seeds and oil. It is often self-sown and can become established in the bush along water-courses. The strong pithy stems grow up to 3 m tall. The leaves are toothed, and the surface of the plant is rough. The flower heads are large, with a centre of tubular flowers and yellow petals formed by ray flowers. There are several rows of bracts around the head. These have rough edges. There are chaffy scales on the disc, as well as the crown of scales at the top of each seed. The seeds are large, flat and oval with pointed ends.

The name *helianthus* comes from the Greek word *helios* meaning *the sun,* and *anthos* meaning *flower.*

Genus *Wedelia* (Sunflower daisies)

Wedelias have a flower head with central tubular flowers and petal-forming ray flowers. There are scales on the disc (base of the flower head). The seed has no bristles, but is crowned with a tiny ring.

Wedelia stirlingii (Sunflower daisy)

This scented daisy is often found in rocky gorges, and is seen at Standley Chasm. It grows 30 cm-1 m high, with pithy erect stems. The surface is rough to touch. The leaves are stiff, rough and often toothed. The yellow petals are about 1 cm long. The seed has a tiny crown and is often winged.

Wedelia stirlingii (Sunflower daisy)

W. asperimma (Sunflower daisy)

This is very similar to *W. stirlingii*, but the seeds differ. It grows to the north of Alice Springs, and is known as a stock poison. The name comes from the Latin word *asper* meaning *rough*.

Genus *Senecio* (Groundsells, Yellowtops)

Senecios are characterised by having a seed-head of silky white feathery bristles. The name *senecio* comes from a Latin word *senex* meaning *an old man*, and refers to the seed-head. The flower head has a centre of yellow tubular flowers and may or may not have petals. If there are petals they are usually not numerous.

Senecio gregorii (Annual yellowtop)

Yellowtop provides one of the unforgetable sights of Central Australia. When there are good autumn or winter rains these yellow starry daisies carpet the countryside in spring. In dry years there may be none. Yellowtop is a fleshy hairless annual which grows about 30 cm tall. The heads have a yellow

centre and 7-8 petals. The centre is 1 cm wide and the petals up to 2 cm long. The petals are spaced out, giving the daisy a star-like shape. The calyx is a bell-shaped tube. The leaves are alternate, and not toothed. The seed-head is composed of fine silky white bristles.

Senecio gregorii (Annual yellowtop)

Senecio gregorii (Annual yellowtop) seed-head

S. magnificus (Perennial yellowtop, Tall yellowtop, Camel weed)

The name *magnificus* means *magnificent* or *splendid*. Tall yellowtop is a hairless woody perennial about 1 m tall. The toothed fleshy leaves clasp the stem. The flower heads are in clusters. They have a yellow centre, and 8 or so yellow petals 1-2 cm long. The seeds have feathery crowns typical of *Senecio*. This plant is found in floodout areas and along roadsides, but also on open plains.

S. lautus (Elegant yellowtop)

The name *lautus* means *elegant*. Elegant yellowtop is very like *S. gregorii*. It differs in that the flower heads are in clusters, the flower cup (calyx) has separate bracts, and the leaves are toothed or divided.

S. laceratus and S. cunninghamii

These also occur in CA-NT. They are both without petals, having only tubular flowers in the head.

Senecio magnificus (Perennial yellowtop, Tall yellowtop, Camel weed)

Genus *Myriocephalus*

In this genus, the flower heads are hemispherical with a large centre and rows of papery petals. The centre is made up of tubular flowers which are arranged in groups to form smaller heads within the main head. The name *myriocephalus* means *many heads*. The petals are formed by the papery bracts. The seed is silky, each with a crown of 1-13 feathery bristles.

Myriocephalus stuartii (Poached egg daisy)

Poached egg daisy is an annual which grows in deep sand and appears after good autumn or winter rains. The flower heads are on long graceful stems, with the hairy grey-green leaves near the base of the plant. The heads are 2-4 cm in diameter.

Myriocephalus stuartii (Poached egg daisy)

M. rudallii (Small poached egg daisy)

M. rudallii is found to the north of Alice Springs. It is a smaller plant, with branches which lie on the ground before turning upwards. The flower heads are only up to 1.5 cm in diameter.

Myriocephalus stuartii (Poached egg daisy)

Genus *Calocephalus* (billybuttons)

The name *calocephalus* comes from the Greek words *kalos* meaning *beautiful* and *kephalus* meaning *heads*. The yellow flower heads can be conical or flattened. There are no petals. Each head contains 10-100 smaller heads. The seed has a crown of 6-15 feathery bristles with a ring at the base. There are 15 species. They are found only in Australia. There are 2 in CA-NT.

Calocephalus platycephalus (Yellow billybutton)

The word *platycephalus* means *flat heads*. This perennial is only one of the plants which are commonly called billybuttons. In *C. platycephalus* the compound yellow heads are globular with a flattened top, and are 1-3 cm wide. The smaller heads are distinct and each have 12-25 flowers. The stems and leaves are white-woolly, the leaves up to 3 cm long. The small warty seeds have 6-10 feathery bristles.

Calocephalus platycephalus (Yellow billybutton)

C. knappii (Billybutton)

This has yellow-orange to brown flower heads which are globular or pear-shaped, and 8-15 mm wide. The smaller heads are not distinct. Each has 7-15 flowers. The stems and leaves are white-woolly, and the leaves are up to 2 cm long.

Genus *Craspedia* (billybuttons)

Craspedia species have compound yellow heads with numerous partial heads each with only 3-10 flowers. There are no petals, the seeds are silky, with a feathery crown of bristles.

Craspedia pleiocephala (Soft billybutton)

The word *pleiocephala* means *more than one head*. This sparsely-hairy erect annual grows 5-30 cm tall. The heads are pear-shaped and the smaller heads have 3-5 flowers.

Calocephalus knappii (billybutton)

C. chrysantha (Golden billybutton)

This small annual is similar to C. *pleiocephala*, but it has a grey woolly covering.

Genus *Chryscoryne*

Chryscoryne pusilla (Dwarf cup flower)

This very small erect annual grows only 3-12 cm high. The stems are fine and stiff (like copper wire) so that the heads dance in the breeze. The compound yellow heads are narrow-ellipsoid. The seed has a tiny ring at the top. This species is found in low-lying salty areas.

Genus *Gnephosis*

These annuals also have compound heads. There are 3 species found in CA-NT.

Gnephosis skirrophora

This species has heads which are oblong or pear-shaped. The plant has erect stems only 3-20 cm high. The seed is crowned by a small cup 1 mm long.

Gnephosis skirrophora

Chriscoryne pusilla (Dwarf cup flower)

Genus *Rutidosis* (wrinkleworts)

Rutidosis are much-branched perennials with hemispherical flower heads, and no petals. The bracts are yellow. The seed is shaped like an inverted cone, and has a crown of spade-like scales. There are 10 species, found only in Australia, one in CA-NT.

Rutidosis helichrysoides (Grey wrinklewort)

This is a hairy grey-green perennial 25-50 cm high. The narrow leaves run back along the stem where they are attached. The plant can readily be identified by its flower and seed.

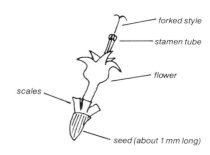

Rutidosis helichrysoides (Grey wrinklewort) – seed

forked style

stamen tube

flower

scales

seed (about 1 mm long)

Genus *Waitzia*

Waitzias are annuals which are usually seen after good winter rain. The distinctive flowers have many rows of yellow or orange petal-like bracts. The flowers are shorter than the bracts. The small seed has a brush of feathery or barbed bristles carried on a stalk-like filament. Waitzias are native to Australia only.

Waitzia acuminata (Orange immortelle)

This is a small shrub 30-60 cm high, which is covered with short soft hairs. The thick narrow leaves are 1-7 cm long. The bell-shaped flower heads are up to 7 x 1.5 cm. There are several rows of yellow or orange petal-like bracts which are fringed and stalked.

W. citrina (Pale immortelle)

This small slightly woolly shrub grows about 20-30 cm high. The hemispherical flower heads are white or yellow, and 5-10 mm wide. The inner bracts are stalked but the outer ones are not.

Waitzia acuminata (Orange immortelle)

Genus *Podolepis*

Podolepis are found only in Australia. There are about 20 species, 2 in CA-NT.

Podolepis canescens (Grey podolepis)

Grey podolepis grows erect, 10-80 cm tall. The stems are fine and stiff, resembling copper wire, and tend to be woolly. The leaves are 2-8 cm long, and mostly on the stems. The yellow flower heads have both disc and ray flowers. The soft petals are 6-10 mm long. The seed is warty, with 25-35 bristles.

P. capillaris (Wiry podolepis)

This small erect annual is 10-60 cm high. It is wiry and waxy, and almost hairless. The leaves are about 1-4 cm x 1 mm, and are mainly on the stems. Being very narrow they are often not noticeable. The flower heads are white. The petals are 3 lobed and about 2.5 mm long. The seed has 15-18 barbed bristles.

Podolepis canescens (Grey podolepis)

Paper Daisies

Helichrysum and *Helipterum* are genera which have papery 'petals'. These two are very similar and were originally grouped together as *Helichrysum*. The name *helichrysum* comes from Greek words: *helios* meaning *the sun,* and *khrysos* meaning *gold.* The flower heads have a centre of yellow tubular flowers surrounded by several rows of overlapping papery bracts, which may form papery petals. The seeds are crowned by slender bristles. In *Helipterum* these bristles are feathery from base to apex. The name *helipterum* comes from *pteron,* the Greek word for *feather.* In *Helichrysum* the bristles are not feathery at the base, but may be feathery or bristly at the apex.

Podolepis capillaris (Wiry podolepis)

216

Genus *Helichrysum*

There are about 500 species of *Helichrysum*. The majority are in Europe and the Middle East. There are 11 found in CA-NT.

Helichrysum semifertile

This is a small everlasting daisy with white petals 2-5 mm long, and a yellow centre. It grows only 20 cm high.

H. *bracteatum* (Golden everlasting)

This daisy is widespread throughout Australia. The stiff strong heads dry well, and are frequently used in dried-flower arrangements. The plant is an erect perennial which is hairy, and rough to touch. The leaves are soft and fleshy, about 4-12 cm long. The heads have a yellow centre and stiff golden petals. The outer bracts may be reddish-brown. The seed has a crown of fine yellow bristles.

Helichrysum bracteatum (Golden everlasting)

H. *davenportii* (Davenport daisy)

This everlasting is an annual, and so is seen after winter rains. The heads are on individual erect stems. They have a yellow centre, and pink petals up to 2 cm long. The leaves are clustered at the base of the plant. The plant surface is rough and hairy. The seed is 8-12 mm long, with over 50 long fine bristles.

Helichrysum davenportii (Davenport daisy)

H. cassinianum (Pink everlasting)

This pink everlasting is an annual. The flower heads are in clusters. The outer bracts are golden-brown and membranous, and enclose a cylindrical head. The pink papery petals are 1 cm long, and can be seen as prolongations from the bracts. The densely hairy leaves are at the base and along the stems. The seed is up to 6 mm long, and has a crown of long fine bristles.

H. apiculatum (Small yellow button)

This perennial daisy is found throughout Australia. It grows 20-60 cm high. The foliage looks grey because of a dense covering of matted hairs. The small yellow globular flower heads are about 1 cm wide, and are in clusters on the ends of stems. The heads have no petals, but are surrounded by rows of overlapping golden-yellow bracts. The small warty seed has a crown of 6-12 bristles.

H. thomsonii (Thomson's daisy)

This perennial daisy is found in rocky places such as Kings Canyon and Glen Helen, and is often seen high up on rock-faces. The bottom part of the stem is woody. The leaves are large and pointed, up to 7.5 x 2.5 cm. They are markedly reticulated, and densely hairy and glandular. The flower heads are in clusters. The heads are about 1 cm wide, with a yellow centre and white papery petals.

Helichrysum apiculatum (Small yellow button)

Helichrysum thomsonii (Thomson's daisy)

Helichrysum cassinianum (Pink everlasting)

Genus *Helipterum*

There are about 100 species of *Helipterum* found in Africa and Australia, 12 in CA-NT.

Helipterum fitzgibbonii (Fitzgibbon's daisy)

Fitzgibbon's daisy is a graceful annual 7-45 cm tall. The flower heads are held erect, nodding on delicate stems. They have yellow centres, white papery petals, and a purplish-brown bell-shaped back. The yellow flowers in the centre are surrounded by many rows of bracts. The outside bracts are purple-brown with frilled edges. Inside these are the bracts which form the white petals. The innermost bracts have small blades with white woolly stalks. The seed has a crown of 8-13 feathery bristles.

H. floribundum (White paper daisy)

This much-branched many-flowered daisy is usually 10-20 cm high though it can be taller. The stems and leaves are grey-green due to hairiness. The flower heads are 1-2 cm wide, hemispherical, with yellow centres and white paper petals.

Helipterum fitzgibbonii (Fitzgibbon's daisy)

Helipterum floribundum (White paper daisy)

H. stipitatum (Saltspoon daisy)

The word *stipitatum* means *stalked*, and refers to the stalked yellow bracts which form the petals of this flower head. These bracts are shaped like tiny saltspoons, hence the common name. Saltspoon daisy is a hairy grey-green annual which grows 30-40 cm high. The flower heads are on long spreading stems, with leaves mainly at the lower half of the plant. The yellow heads are up to 3 cm wide.

H. pterochaetum (Perennial sunray)

This much-branched small shrub has small yellow flower heads, without petals. The conical heads are only 3-5 mm wide. They are on stalks and grouped loosely into clusters. The narrow leaves are sticky and have rolled edges. The stems are white-woolly. The seeds have feathery bristles. The name *pterochaetum* comes from the words *pteros* meaning *a feather* and *chaetum* meaning *a bristle*.

Helipterum stipitatum (Saltspoon daisy)

Helipterum pterochaetum (Perennial sunray)

H. charsleyae (Charles daisy)

The spelling *charsleyae* is the result of a mistake in recording the original description. Charles daisy grows about 30 cm tall, and is hairless or nearly so, and this distinguishes it from other similar daisies. The stalked yellow cylindrical flower heads are 2-6 mm wide, and held closely in clusters. There are no petals. The outer bracts are straw-coloured, and the inner are yellow. The silky-haired seed has 12-22 bristles.

H. tietkinsii (Sand sunray, Tietkin's daisy)

Sand sunray is a small greyish plant with a hairy surface. The yellow flower heads have no petals. They are small, cylindrical, 3-6 mm wide, and clustered together without stalks. The bracts have a green midrib. The seed is not wrapped in wool as is that of musk daisy.

H. moschatum (Musk daisy)

This is very similar to *H. tietkinsii*, but it has a cottony wool enveloping the seed.

Helipterum tietkinsii (Tietkin's daisy)

Helipterum charsleyae (Charles daisy)

Genus *Pterocaulon*

Pterocaulons are perennial daisies with compound flower heads each containing many smaller heads. There are no petals. The leaves form wings where they join the stem. The name *pterocaulon* comes from the Greek *pteron* meaning *a wing,* and *kaulos* meaning *a stem.* There are 6 species in Australia, 2 in CA-NT.

Pterocaulon sphacelatum (Apple bush)

This small twiggy bush has pink and white globular flower heads. In the compound head smaller heads can be seen, each with one large tubular flower in the centre. The plant is glandular-hairy, and has a strong scent of apples. The leaves are toothed except on the wings. The tiny seed has a dense crown of fine bristles. This species is very widespread in CA-NT. Being a perennial, it responds quickly to moisture.

Pterocaulon sphacelatum (Apple bush)

P. serrulatum (Apple bush)

This small scented shrub is similar to *P. sphacelatum.* The glandular-hairy leaves are toothed, including the wings. The compound heads are oblong, 2-3.5 cm long. There are variants in this species.

Liliaceae (lily family)

Lilies are perennials which die back and shoot annually. The stems are pithy, not woody, and the leaves are sheathed at the base. The flowers have 3 or 6 segments, which are called tepals, because they cannot be exactly differentiated into petals and sepals. In some lilies all tepals are alike, in others the 3 inner tepals are different. The tepals are often called petals, or petals and sepals. Here they will be called petals. In some species the flowers are tubular or bell-shaped. The fruit is a juicy berry or a dry capsule.

Pterocaulon serrulatum (Apple bush)

222

Lilies are mainly temperate zone plants and not many are found in very dry regions. The family includes vegetables such as asparagus, onion, leek, and garlic, as well as ornamental garden lilies.

Genus *Wurmbea* (Early Nancy) – also called *Anguillaria*

Wurmbea deserticola (Early Nancy)

This Early Nancy is found in moist places after rain. The plants are lily-like, 20-25 cm high, with sheathed fleshy leaves (some of them dilated at the base) up to 10 x 1 cm in size. The star-shaped flowers are in erect spikes containing 3-11 flowers and are pink with red markings at the base of the petals. The Aborigines are said to have eaten the bulbs.

W. centralis (Early Nancy)

This is found only at Mt Olga. It is similar to *W. deserticola*, but there are slight differences in the flowers.

Wurmbea centralis (Early Nancy)

Genus *Caesia*

Caesia lateriflora (Sand lily)

Sand lily is often seen on sand-dunes, as a tangled mass of fine smooth branching stems which develop each year from tuberous roots. The grass-like leaves grow from the base and wither before the flowers come. The yellow-green flowers are only 4-6 mm long, and are on short stalks at the angles of the stems. The flowering period is brief, and the fruits which develop are small nuts.

Caesia lateriflora (Sand lily)

Genus *Thysanotus*

Thysanotus exiliflorus (Fringe lily)

T. exiliflorus is very like *T. tuberosus* (the common fringe lily). The name *thysanotus* is the Greek word for *fringed*. *T. exiliflorus* is a perennial, with fibrous roots which expand into tubers some distance from the plant. It shoots annually and the leaves wither before flowering. The flower-stem grows 8-19 cm tall, with diverging branches.

The flowers are lilac, with 3 broad fringed inner petals (tepals) and 3 narrow petals which are not fringed. The petals are 7-12 mm long. The globular seed-capsule is enclosed in the persistent petals, and the black seeds have orange stalks. The tubers were roasted and eaten by the Aborigines.

Thysanotus exiliflorus (Fringe lily)

224

Genus *Bulbine*

Bulbine semibarbata (Leek lily)

Leek lily has a root which is fibrous but not tuberous. The leaves are long, narrow and strap-like, up to 20 cm long. The flowers are yellow with petals 4-6 mm long.

Genus *Arthropodium*

Arthropodium strictum (Chocolate lily)

This lily has blue, white or lilac flowers with petals 10-12 mm long. The flowers are chocolate scented.

Genus *Crinum*

There are about 10 species of *Crinum* in Australia.

Crinum flaccidum (Darling lily, Murray lily)

This is a tall perennial lily with a bulbous root, long strap-like leaves, and the flowers in a cluster at the end of a strong stem. The white flowers are strongly scented and consist of a narrow tube widening into 6 broad flaring petals. The fruit is a capsule. The bulbs are edible and have been used in the past to make a cornflour substitute.

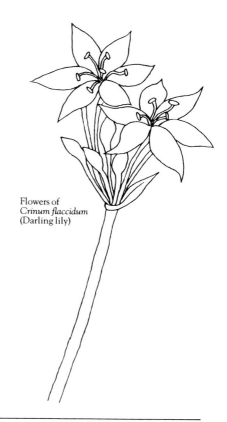

Flowers of
Crinum flaccidum
(Darling lily)

Xanthorrhoeaceae
(grass-tree family)

This group have long narrow leaves which form tussocks. The leaves are hard and rush-like. The flowers are in scattered clusters or on long spikes.

Genus *Xanthorrhoea* (grass-trees or blackboys)

There are about 15 species of grass-tree found in Australia. They are really neither grass nor tree, but are related to the lily. The part above ground is long-lived; it consists of a fibrous trunk topped by a large tuft of long hard leaves. The flowers are in a spike up to 4 m long. In some parts of Australia the resin obtained from the trunk was widely used commercially: in varnishes, stove polish, the manufacture of picric acid, and to produce gas, tar and coke. It has only limited commercial use today.

Xanthorrhoea thorntonii (Desert grass-tree)

This is found only in a few places in CA and one part of WA. A group can be seen near Gosse's Bluff, and also in the George Gill Ranges near Kings Canyon. The leaves are numerous: long, narrow, stiff and pointed, and up to 1.5 m long and 2 mm square in cross-section. The numerous creamy-white flowers are in a dense spike up to 4 m long. The Aborigines used resin from the trunk as an adhesive and also obtained honey from the flowers.

Xanthorrhoea thorntonii (Desert grass-tree)

Arecaceae (palm family)
– also called Palmae

Genus *Livistona*

Livistona mariae (Central Australian cabbage palm)

There are many species of cabbage palm found in Australia. The stand of *L. mariae* which is found in the Palm Valley region of CA is restricted to 60 square kilometres on the Finke River and its tributaries. It is a remnant from millions of years ago when CA was much wetter and covered by such vegetation. This stand has remained because of the unique geological nature of the area, in which water continually seeps down from the tops of the gorges into the rocky shales beneath. The trees have erect trunks which are topped by divided palm-like leaves on long strong stems.

The small flowers are in branching clusters which hang beneath the canopy, and the globular fruits are 1-2 cm in diameter. Young seedlings are pink in colour. It is thought that mature trees may be up to 300 years old. Although there is present evidence of good growth of young trees, survival of the species depends on the protection of the unique environment.

Livistona mariae (Central Australian cabbage palm)

Livistona mariae (Central Australian cabbage palm) seedling

GLOSSARY

affinity – in classifications, a relationship based either on genetic make-up or physical make-up.

anther – the part of the stamen containing pollen.

angular – sharp-cornered.

barb – a short rigid hair which is often hooked.

beak – a terminal projection.

beard – a tuft or tufts of hairs.

berry – a pulpy or fleshy fruit which does not open to release the seeds.

bisexual – of flowers, a flower with reproductive organs of both sexes.

bladder – an inflated, usually hollow structure.

blade – of a leaf, the flattened part.

bract – a leaf-like structure at the base of a flower or flower-head.

bracteole – an accessory bract.

bristle – a stiff hair.

bud – a cell or group of cells with potential for producing vegetative or reproductive growth.

bulb, bulbous roots – a short thick rootstock in which the buds are covered by leaf scales.

burr – a rough barbed spiny or prickly fruit which encloses the seeds.

calyx – the first whorl of a flower, formed by a number of sepals, which can be either joined in a cup or separate.

capsule – a dry fruit which opens by valves or pores.

cilia (singular-**cilium**) – fine soft hairs, usually part of a fringe.

compound – composed of several parts.
        – of a leaf, having several leaflets.
        – of a flower-head, having several to many smaller or partial flower-heads.

decoction – the liquor obtained by boiling a substance in water to extract the soluble substances.

disc – a thickening of the end of the receptacle. (The receptacle is the thickened end of the flower-stalk.)

elliptic – of a leaf, a flat surface which tapers evenly towards each end.

epicalyx – a whorl of leafy segments at the base of the calyx, forming an outer calyx.

filament – a thread-like structure.
        – in a stamen, the stalk carrying the anther.

flower-head – as in a wattle or daisy, a large number of small unstalked flowers closely held together on top of a single stalk.

flower-spike – a group of flowers arranged along a terminal flower stem, used here to describe unstalked flowers and also flowers with short stalks. Botanically the term refers to unstalked flowers arranged on a stem.

follicle – a fruiting capsule which splits open to release the seeds.

frond – the leaf of a fern, also used for a palm leaf.

fruit – the ripe seeds plus the structures surrounding them.

fruiting-body – of a fern, the sexually reproductive structure.

genus (plural-**genera**) – in classification, a grouping of closely related species within a family. A family usually has a number of genera which each have a number of species.

gland – a wart-like structure which usually secretes a fluid.

hair – of a plant, an outgrowth from the outer layers of the epidermis. Hairs have various shapes and functions. Star-shaped hairs are formed when several hairs radiate from one point. They look star-shaped under magnification.

herb – a plant whose stem does not become woody.

hybrid – progeny of cross-fertilisation between two species.

hybridisation – the production of a hybrid from 2 different species, such that there is a genetic mix.

inflated – enlarged or swollen.

involucre – the rings of bracts surrounding a flower or flower-head.

keel – in pea flowers, the 2 lower petals united in the shape of the keel of a boat.
   – in general, a ridge on a fold in a leaf, bract, or other plant part, shaped like a boat keel.

lanceolate – tapering to each end and broadest at the end nearest the stalk.

leaf – **simple leaf** – not divided into lobes or leaflets.
   – **divided leaf** – a leaf with separated parts.
   – **compound leaf** – a leaf consisting of an arrangement of leaflets.

leaflet – a segment of a compound leaf. Each leaflet looks like an entire leaf.

lignotuber – in members of the myrtle family including eucalypts, a swelling at the base of the stem, at or below the ground, which has dormant buds which can initiate new growth.

lobe – a part of a leaf, flower or calyx which is separated but not divided completely to its origin. A lobe usually means a rounded projection, but in plant parts it may be narrow and pointed.

mallee – in eucalypts, a type of growth where several trunks arise from a lignotuber.

membranous – thin, delicate, and translucent.

nectary – a gland secreting nectar.

node – of a stem, joint of a stem, from which a leaf arises.

nut – a dry fruit containing one seed and not opening when ripe.

operculum – in eucalypts, a cap on the bud, formed by the petals and/or sepals.

ovary – the female chamber which contains the ovules which after fertilisation become the seeds.

ovate – of a leaf, egg-shaped in outline, with tapered ends, and wider at the basal end.
    – **obovate** leaf, similar but wider at the far end.

ovoid – egg-shaped or pear-shaped, attached at the wider end.

pappus – a tuft of bristles, hairs or feathery components.
    – in a daisy, the bristles or scales arising at the top of the ovary in place of a calyx.

petals – botanical meaning, segments or units of the flower which form the second whorl of floral appendages called the corolla. (The calyx is the first.) Petals may be united in a tube or separate.
    – in this work the word petal is also used to describe petal-like parts which are not true petals. These may be bracts, tepals, rays or lobes.

phyllode – a leaf-like stalk which functions as a leaf.

pith – the spongy material in the centre of some plant stems.
    – the spongy tissue in some fruits.

pod – a fruit characteristic of the legumes and also some of the cabbage family. The pod splits open when mature.

pore – a minute opening in the plant epidermis, used for transpiration and gas exchange.

ray – of a daisy-head, the long petal-like projection from the outmost flowers of the flower-head.

receptacle – of a flower, the end of the flower-stem to which the floral whorls are attached.
    – of a flower-head, the structure at the end of the stem, to which the flowers are attached.

***Rhizobium* bacteria** – a gram negative aerobic bacillus of which certain species are found in root nodules of leguminous plants, where they fix nitrogen from the air in the soil so that it can be absorbed by the plant. Each plant species requires a particular strain of the bacteria.

rhizome – an underground root.

rootstock – the mainly underground part at the base of the plant, capable of producing new growth each year.

scales – of leaves, membranous reduced leaves.
    – of daisy flower-heads, a tiny thin chaffy structure attached to the disc between the flowers.

sepals – a component part of the first whorl (outer whorl) of the flower. The petals are the component parts of the second whorl. The sepals together make up the calyx.

sheath – a tubular structure formed by the leaf and encircling the stem.

species – a related group of individuals with similar genetic make-up and growth patterns, which breed freely together but do not breed freely with other species.

spore – the single-celled stage in the life-cycle of a fern.

stamen – the male part of the flower, consisting of the anther which contains the pollen and usually a filament, the fine hair-like stalk of the anther.

staminode – an infertile and often much reduced stamen.

standard – of a pea flower, the upper petal, which is usually the largest.

star-shaped hairs – see **hair.**

stigma – the receptive tip of the style, which traps the pollen.

striated – marked with parallel longitudinal lines, grooves or ridges.

style – that part of the female reproductive system which connects the ovary to the stigma. When a pollen grain is accepted it forms a tube down through the style to the ovary.

subspecies – in classification, a minor category below the level of a species.

tepal – a unit of the flower, either sepal or petal. Tepal is usually used when sepals and petals are similar.

terete – circular in cross-section.

tessellated – marked in a pattern of squares.

tribe – a grouping of several genera within a family.

tuber, tuberous roots – a large swelling on a root or underground stem, which contains food reserves and may have growth buds.

valves – parts into which the wall of a fruit may split to release the seeds.

variety – a minor category below a species, a group of individuals with genetic similarity and a restricted geographic range, which maintain a distinction within the species. The term subspecies is often used interchangeably with variety.

vegetative reproduction – reproducing asexually – by cuttings, suckers, buds, etc.

warty – knobbly.

wings – in general a wing is a thin, flat and usually dry or membranous expansion.
    – in a pea flower, the wings are the 2 lateral petals.

REFERENCES

Askew K. and **Mitchell A. S.** (1978) *The Fodder Trees and Shrubs of the Northern Territory.* Extension Bulletin No. 16, Division of Primary Industry. Government Printer of the N.T., Darwin.

Black J. M. (1978) *Flora of South Australia.* Part I (Third Edition). Revised and edited by John P. Jessop. Government Printer: South Australia.

Black J. M. (1948-52) *Flora of South Australia.* Parts II and III (Second Edition). Government Printer: South Australia.

Black J. M. (1965) *Flora of South Australia.* Part IV (Second Edition). Revised by Enid L. Robertson. Government Printers: Adelaide, S.A.

Chippendale G. M. and **Jephcott B. R.** (1963) *Topfeed – The Fodder Trees and Shrubs of Central Australia.* Northern Territory Administration, Animal Industry Branch. Extension Article No. 5. Government Printer, Adelaide.

Chippendale G. M. and **Murray L. R.** (1963) *Poisonous Plants of the Northern Territory.* Northern Territory Administration, Animal Industry Branch. Extension Article No. 2. Government Printer, Adelaide.

Cleland J. B. (1966) 'The ecology of the aboriginal in south and central Australia', in *Aboriginal Man in South and Central Australia* (Cotton B. C., editor): pp. 111-158. Government Printer, Adelaide.

Cribb A. B. (1981) *Wild Medicine in Australia.* Collins/Fontana, Sydney.

Cribb A. B. and **J. W.** (1982) *Wild Foods in Australia* (revised edition), Fontana, Sydney.

Cribb A. B. and **J. W.** (1984) *Useful Wild Plants in Australia.* Fontana, Sydney.

Cunningham G. M., Mulham W.E., Milthorpe P.L., and **Leigh J. H.** (1981) *Plants of Western New South Wales.* Soil Conservation Service of N.S.W. Government Printing Office, Sydney.

Debenham C. *The Language of Botany.* The Society for Growing Australian Plants.

Dunlop C. R. (Ed.) (1987) *Checklist of Vascular Plants of the Northern Territory.* Technical Report No. 26. Government Printer, Darwin.

Griffen W. J. (1985) 'Duboisias of Australia', in *Pharmacy International,* December 1985.

Harmer J. *North Australian Plants: Volume I – Wildflowers of the Northern Territory Top End.* The Society for Growing Australian Plants.

Hogkinson K. C. and **Griffen G. F.** (1982) 'Adaptation of shrub species to fires in the arid zone', in *Evolution of the Flora and Fauna of Arid Australia* (Barker W. R., Greenslade P. J. M., editors): pp. 145-152. Peacock Publications in association with the Australian Systematic Botany Society and ANZAAS South Australian Division Inc.

Jessop J. (Ed.) (1981) *Flora of Central Australia.* The Systematic Botany Society. A. H. and A. W. Reed, Sydney.

Latz P. K. (1965) 'Notes on the Relict Palm *Livistona Mariae.* F. MUELL. In Central Australia', from *Transactions of the Royal Society of South Australia.* Vol. 99, Pt. 4, pp. 189-196.

Maconochie J. R. (1982) 'Regeneration of arid zone plants: a floristic survey', in *Evolution of the Flora and Fauna of Arid Australia* (Barker W. R., Greenslade P. J. M., editors): pp. 141-144. Peacock Publications in association with the Australian Systematic Botany Society and ANZAAS South Australian Division Inc.

Mitchell A. S. (1980) *Eucalypts of Central Australia.* Conservation Commission of the Northern Territory. Technical Bulletin No. 3. C.C.N.T., Alice Springs.

New T. R. (1984) *A Biology of Acacias.* Oxford University Press in association with Latrobe University Press, Melbourne.

Noble J. C. (1982) 'The significance of fire in the biology and evolutionary ecology of mallee Eucalyptus populations', in *Evolution of the Flora and Fauna of Arid Australia* (Barker, Greenslade, editors) pp. 153-159. Peacock Publications in association with the Australian Systematic Botany Society and ANZAAS South Australian Division Inc.

Payne W. H. (managing editor) (1985) 'Wildflowers of Central Australia,' *Australian Plants* Vol. 13, No. 103, pp. 94-139 (June 1985). Society for Growing Australian Plants.

Raven P. H. and **Evert R. F.** (1981) *Biology of Plants* (Third Edition). Worth Publishers, New York.

Simmons M. H. (1981) *Acacias of Australia.* Thomas Nelson Australia, Melbourne.

Strong B. W. *Checklist of Preferred Common names of Plants of the Northern Territory,* Government Printer, Darwin.

Watson P. L., Luanratana O., and **Griffen W. J.** (1983) 'The Ethnopharmacology of Pituri' in *Journal of Ethnopharmacology* 8, (1983) pp. 303-311. Elsevier Scientific Publishers Ireland Ltd.

Wauchope J. (1978) *Ormiston Gorge and Pound National Park.* Territory Parks and Wildlife, N.T. Government.

INDEX

BOTANICAL AND COMMON NAMES

NOTES